Potter's Raid through South Carolina

The Final Days of the Confederacy

Tom Elmore

Published by The History Press
Charleston, SC 29403
www.historypress.net

Copyright © 2015 by Tom Elmore
All rights reserved

First published 2015

Front cover, top: General Edward Potter. *From the Military Order of the Loyal Legion of the United States Collection, U.S. Army Heritage and Education Center, Carlisle, Pennsylvania.*

Front cover, bottom: General William T. Sherman on his famed March to the Sea. General Potter's raid in South Carolina was much like that of Sherman's in Georgia, as Potter and his men were tasked with destroying supplies in the South Carolina Sandhills. *Courtesy of the Library of Congress.*

Manufactured in the United States

ISBN 978.1.62619.959.0

Library of Congress CIP data applied for.

Notice: The information in this book is true and complete to the best of our knowledge. It is offered without guarantee on the part of the author or The History Press. The author and The History Press disclaim all liability in connection with the use of this book.

All rights reserved. No part of this book may be reproduced or transmitted in any form whatsoever without prior written permission from the publisher except in the case of brief quotations embodied in critical articles and reviews.

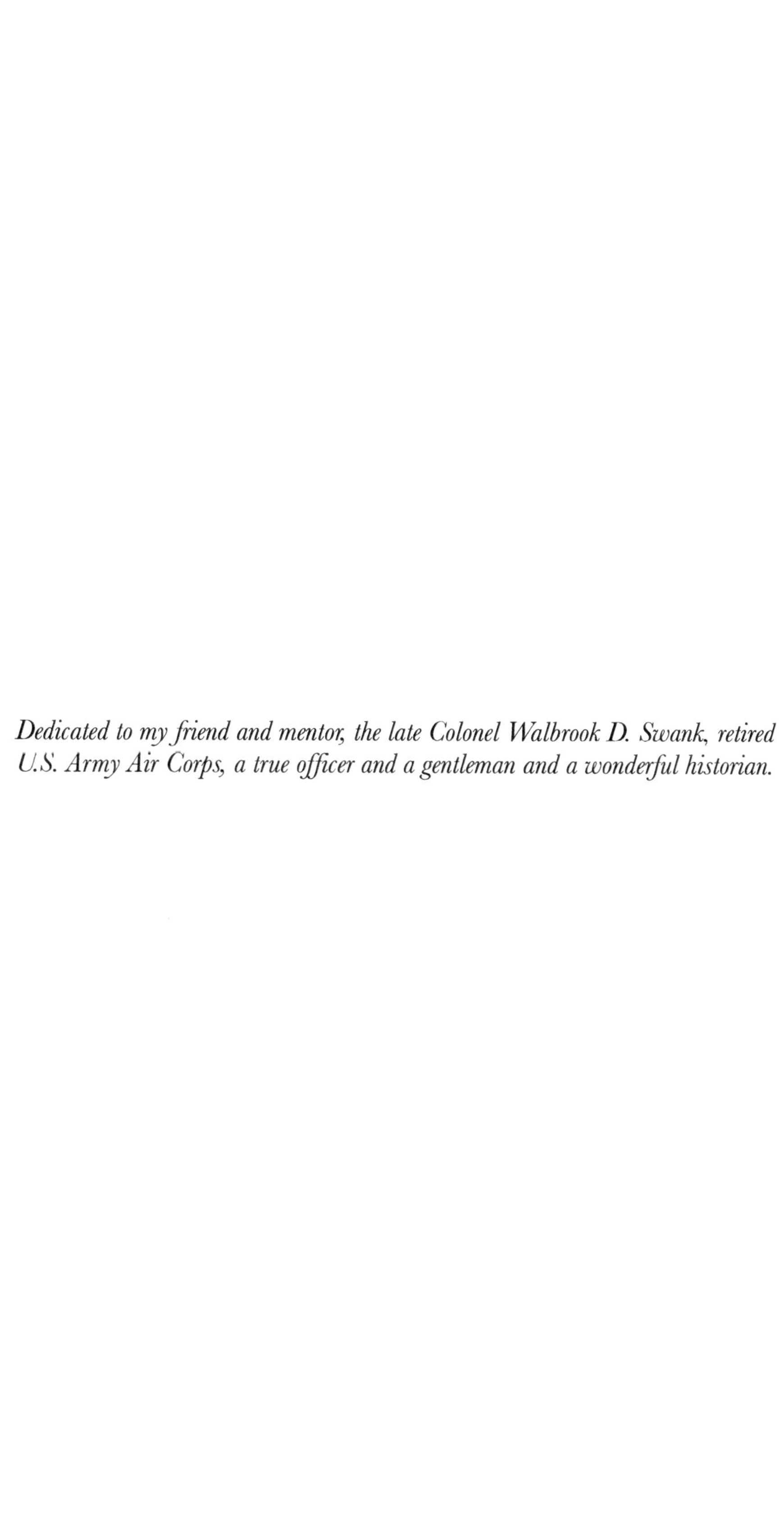

Dedicated to my friend and mentor, the late Colonel Walbrook D. Swank, retired U.S. Army Air Corps, a true officer and a gentleman and a wonderful historian.

Contents

Acknowledgements

I would like to thank the staffs of the following institutions for helping to make this book possible:

South Carolina Confederate Relic Room and Military Museum, Columbia, SC
South Carolina Department of Archives and History, Columbia, SC
South Caroliniana Library, University of South Carolina, Columbia, SC
Sumter County Historical Commission, Sumter, SC
Thomas Cooper Library, University of South Carolina, Columbia, SC
Walker Local and Family History Center, Richland Library, Columbia, SC

Thanks also to Robert L. Brown, senior lecturer of English at the University of South Carolina–Sumter and member of the Sumter County Historical Commission, for reviewing the manuscript and offering invaluable suggestions, tips, advice and guidance; Chad Rhoad of The History Press, for his continued support of my bringing little-known aspects of South Carolina's nineteenth-century history to light in the twenty-first century; my mother-in-law, Pat Wood, for proofreading the manuscript; my wife, my cheerleader and my princess, Krys Wood-Elmore, for her love and support and for putting up with me being at the computer at strange hours of the day; and Speedy and Sassy, for their constant vigil to protect me from loud noises.

Introduction

In 1886, Reverend William W. Mood wrote in the Sumter, South Carolina *Watchman and Southron*:

> *This march of* [Brigadier General Edward] *Potter* will never be forgotten *because of its atrocities. Much,* very much, *must ever remain* an unwritten history. Their brutality and savage wickedness can never be written. *It was a time of terror.*[1] [emphasis original]

Time has proven the reverend wrong.

When people think about the Civil War—or the War Between the States, depending on loyalties—they usually think about big battles like Gettysburg, Shiloh or Fredericksburg; famous campaigns like the Siege of Vicksburg, the March to the Sea or the Campaign of the Carolinas; or famous generals like Lee, Grant, Jackson and Sherman. However, no war is limited to famous battles, campaigns or generals that have become household names. Indeed, for every famous person or event of the Civil War, there are at least ten lesser-known ones.

This is the story of one of those lesser-known campaigns, Potter's Raid, which took place in April 1865, most of it after Lee surrendered his army to Grant. Even with the Civil War still fresh in people's minds, this raid received scant attention outside the area where it happened. Only a couple stories about it appeared in *Confederate Veteran*, the official publication of the United Confederate Veterans, during its original run of 1893 to 1932. The original series of the *Southern Historical Society Papers*, published between 1876 and 1910, referred to it only once in passing in a biography. Likewise, 1897's *Century Magazine*'s *Battles and Leaders of the Civil War* series has no stories of the raid at all. Even Confederate general turned Episcopal bishop Ellison Capers makes no mention at all of it in his 1899 book, *Confederate Military History: Volume Five, South Carolina*.

Therefore, it should not be surprising that modern scholars have rarely discussed Potter's Raid. The 1941 Works Project Administration *Guide to South Carolina* referred to it only in passing. Dr. Charles Edward Cauthen, in his 1950 study of Palmetto State Civil War politics, *South Carolina Goes to War: 1860–1865*, ignored it completely. A 1964 biography of the highest-ranking Confederate combatant, Major General Pierce Young, makes no mention of his involvement in the raid, while Dr. Walter Edgar, in his critically acclaimed 1998 book, *South Carolina: A History*, devoted only one paragraph to the event.[2]

Though the raid is at best a side note to the war and an epilogue to Sherman's invasion of South Carolina, for those who participated and those civilians who were unlucky to be in the raiders' path, it was just as terrifying and dramatic as any campaign of the war, leaving scars that have yet to fully heal. Conversely, for the soldiers doing the fighting, their days and nights were filled with uncertainty about what the enemy would do and whether it would be their last day on earth.

This is their story.

Chapter 1

Background of the Raid and the Raiders

The origins of the last Civil War campaign in the state that started the war lies in one of the few failures of Major General William T. Sherman's invasion of South Carolina in the winter of 1865.[3] On March 4 of that year, after Sherman's army had occupied the town of Cheraw, South Carolina, Sherman's second in command and commander of the Federal Army of the Tennessee, Major General Oliver Otis Howard, approached Sherman about sending mounted troops to Florence, South Carolina, to destroy railroad rolling stock before the Confederates could remove it. Sherman approved the raid because it would also "divert attention from our real course," which was Fayetteville, North Carolina. Although Sherman had

Major General Oliver Otis Howard, commander, U.S. Army of the Tennessee. The raid on Florence was Howard's idea, and its lack of success irritated him for the rest of his life. *Courtesy of the Library of Congress.*

seen cavalry raids turn into disasters over the last six months, he was not worried; he felt it would be an easy mission, as "it is not probable there is anything of an enemy at Florence."[4]

Howard ordered Colonel Reuben Williams's 12th Indiana Regiment, the 9th Illinois Mounted Infantry, the 29th Missouri Mounted Infantry "and a detachment of the Fifteenth Army Corps foragers, under command of Major Mahon [to] destroy the depots, trestle-work, bridges, &c., as far as Florence, and, if possible, destroy the public buildings and stores at that place, and then return to Cheraw." On March 4, Williams's force of 546 men left at 11:00 a.m. from Cheraw and camped seven miles outside Darlington that night.[5]

The next morning, Williams's force continued toward Florence, destroying the train trestle between Darlington and Dove's Station. In Darlington, the Federals destroyed 250 bales of cotton, the train depot and a printing office. Then, according to Williams:

> *The command immediately proceeded to carry out the instructions received from department headquarters to go to Florence and destroy the depot, rolling stock, &c., at that place. I proceeded steadily forward till I came near where the wagon road crosses the railroad, when a train was discovered coming in the direction of Darlington. The Twenty-ninth Missouri being in the advance immediately deployed on the side of the track for the purpose of capturing it as soon as it came up. The engineer, however, must have discovered us, as the train was turned back to Florence.*[6]

Realizing that the element of surprise was lost, Williams's men rushed into Florence. Two miles outside Florence, "two brigades of [Confederate] cavalry and a regiment of infantry, besides a number of militia or refugees who were at that time in the place" under the command of Brigadier General Beverly H. Robertson were waiting for him.[7]

Major Henry Hitchcock, an aide to Sherman, estimated Robertson's combined forces at three thousand men (six times the size of the Federals), though postwar accounts suggest that the two sides were more evenly matched. However, Williams was worried that the Confederates had "ten pieces of artillery said to have returned from Society Hill to Florence."[8]

Despite the perceived odds, Williams had his men form a line and charge the Confederates. The charge was successful, but when Williams reached the depot, he found Colonel Charles J. Colcock's 3rd South Carolina Cavalry waiting for him with a detachment of Wheeler's cavalry. The Confederates countercharged, forcing Williams to abandon the depot before he could destroy it, even though Colcock had only 180 men to Williams's 400.[9]

Colonel Charles J. Colcock, commander, 3rd South Carolina Cavalry. The Confederate cavalry leader was the only military leader involved in both the Florence raid and Potter's Raid. *Courtesy of the Walker Local History and Family History Center, Richland Library, Columbia, South Carolina.*

Born in 1820, Colcock was described by a commanding officer as "a country gentleman, a gallant soldier, a genial and lovable Carolinian, honored and esteemed throughout the state." Before the war, Colcock had been a plantation owner, an officer of the Bank of the State of South Carolina and the Memphis and Charleston Railroad and involved in the Charleston and Savannah Railroad, despite never having attended college. He also lacked formal military training yet became colonel of the 3rd South Carolina Cavalry by 1862 and remained its commander until war's end, having distinguished himself at the Battle of Honey Hill on November 30, 1864.[10]

Colcock's regiment had been assigned to watch Sherman's right flank, which placed him and his men between Sherman and Charleston, South Carolina, until the Confederates evacuated the city on February 17, 1865.[11]

A long-standing local tradition claims that rescuing the Federal prisoners being held in the Florence Stockade was an objective of the raid. Since the depot and the stockade were only a mile from each other, this is plausible. However, there are no orders for such a rescue mission in the *Official Records*, nor did Sherman or Howard mention such orders in their personal memoirs. But Henry Wright's history of the 6th Iowa Regiment substantiates this claim, as does the diary of Major Charles Wills. If they are correct, then either Williams decided to do this on his own, or it was a last-minute verbal instruction. Regardless, the effort would have been for naught since the prisoners had already been removed on February 15.[12]

The Confederates reinforced their lines while Williams called in his reserves to protect his flanks. While the fighting was going on, a train arrived from Kingsville (modern-day Kingstree) with four hundred Confederate reinforcements and artillery. Their arrival ended any hope Williams had of taking Florence:

> *Finding that I was outflanked and outnumbered by the enemy, and with a force of 400 moving in my rear, I concluded to withdraw the command and at once proceeded to do so. I fell back in good order, leaving the Ninth Illinois to cover the rear and proceeded in the direction of Darlington.*[13]

The Confederates chased Williams, charging his rear flank "two or three times between Florence and Darlington." Williams wanted to rest in

This simple monument at the Florence battle site marks the farthest point of the Union advance. Its claim that the main purpose of the raid was to free prisoners from the Florence Stockade is incorrect. *Photo by the author.*

Darlington and was about to give orders to that effect when he learned that the Confederates were still in pursuit. Williams "at once concluded to fall back to Black Creek, which was immediately done, and the bridges over the stream in my immediate vicinity destroyed."[14]

That did not stop the Confederates. At 8:00 p.m., Williams learned that "the enemy was moving across Black Creek, on my left, in force." Realizing that the Confederates were trying to reach Society Hill, which would cut him off from Cheraw and force "a long march to the left," Williams ordered his exhausted men to mount up and proceed to Society Hill, which they reached about midnight, in order to rejoin the main army. There, he learned that Robertson's men were "a portion of the army, which was cut off from the main army by the capture of Cheraw."[15]

Williams and his men were back with the XV Corps by March 6. The raid was not a complete failure:

> *The results of the expedition may be summed up as follows: The destruction of 500 yards of trestle-work, 2 depots, 11 freight and 4 passenger cars, 4,000 pounds bacon, 80 bushels wheat, 50 sacks corn, 250 bales of cotton, 1 printing office, 1 caisson and battery wagon, 30 stands of small-arms, and the capture of 31 prisoners. Our casualties are 7 wounded and 8 missing. A lieutenant and one man are reported to have been captured at Society Hill on our return.*[16]

Federal XV Corps commander Major General John Logan tried to put a positive spin on the raid, writing that the "expedition returned without having entered Florence on account of the presence of the enemy in considerable force, but Colonel Williams succeeded in destroying most of the bridging and trestling between Cheraw and Florence, and fully accomplished in this respect the design of the expedition."[17]

Howard, though, was "not satisfied with the results, and thinks if more vim had been used, the troops would have accomplished more, [and] at all events, known better what was at Florence than they appear to now," wrote an aide to Howard. Major Wills was even harsher:

> *That expedition to Florence was a failure. Our men got the town but were driven out before they destroyed a thing. I am inclined to think the officers did not do their whole duty. They should have succeeded or lost more blood. Our loss amounted to nothing.*[18]

In fairness to Williams, the plans for the raid did not take into account the possibility that there were Confederates in Florence, nor did Howard believe that Williams might have been outnumbered.

Though Sherman's thoughts on the raid are unknown, he was apparently not impressed; his cavalry attempted no further raids for the reminder of the war. He told his chief of cavalry, Major General Judson Kilpatrick, on March 7, "There is a body of infantry and cavalry left down in the pocket about Florence that might be caught, but it won't pay to chase them—horse flesh is too precious. Keep your horses in the best order for the day when we must have a big fight—not, however, on this turn."[19]

Despite downplaying the failed Florence raid, Sherman could not let the idea of destroying the railroad and its supplies out of his mind. After capturing Fayetteville, North Carolina, and reestablishing communications with the North, Sherman sent a message to Charleston, South Carolina, to Major General Quincy Gilmore, commander of the U.S. Military Department of the South.[20]

Major General William T. Sherman, commander, U.S. Military Division of the Mississippi. After the raid on Florence failed, Sherman ordered a larger expedition into the South Carolina interior. *Courtesy of the Library of Congress.*

Gilmore was born in Ohio in 1825 and graduated from the United States Military Academy (West Point) in 1849. He spent his prewar military career as an instructor at West Point and in Virginia and New York City. He was part of the successful Union capture of Beaufort/Port Royal, South Carolina area in 1862 and is credited for devising the plan for the successful capture of Fort Pulaski, outside Savannah, Georgia, that same year.[21] Gilmore would also see action during the siege of Charleston in 1863. In 1864, he was transferred to Virginia, where he saw action at Bermuda Hundred and the raid on Washington, D.C. He returned to South Carolina in February 1865 as department commander.[22]

Major General Quincy Gilmore, commander, U.S. Military Department of the South. Gilmore played a major role in the capture of Fort Pulaski, outside Savannah, Georgia, and of the Port Royal/Beaufort, South Carolina area. Both played a crucial role in the success of the U.S. Navy's blockade of Southern ports. *Courtesy of the Library of Congress.*

In his letter dated March 15, 1865, Sherman wrote:

> *When at Columbia* [South Carolina] *I had the railroad broken down to Kingsville and the Wateree bridge. Subsequently from Cheraw I aimed to strike Florence, but sent too weak a party, but the enemy himself has destroyed the Pedee* [sic] *bridge, and has on the railroad at Sumterville, and between it and Florence, a vast amount of rolling-stock, the destruction of which is all important, and it should be done before any repairs can be made whereby they can be removed.*
>
> *I want it done at once, and leave you to devise the way. I think 2,500 men lightly equipped with pack mules only, could reach the road either from Georgetown or the Santee bridge. I think also that you can easily make up*

> *that force from Savannah and Charleston. As to the garrisons of those cities, I don't feel disposed to be over generous, and should not hesitate to burn Savannah, Charleston, and Wilmington, or either of them…the expedition I have indicated to Sumterville and Florence has even higher aims. Those cars and locomotives should be destroyed, if to do it costs you 500 men.*
>
> *I know you can get there all the bacon, beef, meat, &c., your command may want, and a good deal of corn meal. The men could march without knapsacks, with a single blanket, and carry eight days' provisions, which, with what is in the country, will feed the command two weeks. Let it be done at once, and select your own point of departure.*[23]

It is somewhat mysterious why Sherman was so passionate about this raid, especially given his thoughts on the Florence raid a week earlier. Certainly he knew that there were few troops left in South Carolina that could have threatened him. In Columbia, Howard was told that there were only 1,450 men in all of South Carolina fit for military duty who were not already serving in the military and that most of the troops that had faced Sherman in the Palmetto State were now in North Carolina with General Joseph Johnston.[24]

More than likely, the failure of the Florence raid gnawed at him and left him frustrated to the point that he could not let it go until the mission was completed, though Sherman would later admit that the return of Johnston to command on February 23 concerned him: "I knew that my special antagonist, General Jos. Johnston, was back with part of his old army [and] that he would not be misled by feints and false reports, and would somehow compel me to exercise more caution than I had hitherto done."[25]

Sherman's suggestion that the cities of Savannah, Charleston and Wilmington be destroyed in order to free up troops is consistent with his impulsive way of talking and doing things. It is doubtful that Gilmore, or anyone else, took seriously the idea of destroying the coastal ports. In fact, the relative lack of field experience of the man who would be the expedition's commander and his troops suggests that the mission was not given the high priority Sherman demanded. Besides, the U.S. Navy would have opposed destroying its newly gained bases of operations.

The obvious point of departure was Georgetown, South Carolina. Founded in 1729, it is the state's third-oldest city. Gilmore had started making plans for the capture of Georgetown in February 1865. On February 21, he contacted Rear Admiral John A. Dahlgren, commander of the South Atlantic Blockading Squadron, about the navy's cooperation in such a move:

Pre–Civil War railroad bed, Sumter County, South Carolina. Per Sherman's orders, the destruction of the railroads and railroad equipment was the main priority of the raiders. *Photo by the author.*

> *I am moving a force out on the Northeastern Railroad toward the Santee River, in order to have supplies there for General Sherman, should he require them. If it be practicable to ascend the Santee River with transports it would*

> *cover my movement and open up even a better line for sending supplies on than the railroad. Could you send some gun-boats up on a reconnaissance in order to get information as to the character of that stream? Deserters report the battery at Georgetown to be abandoned by the enemy. I hope to be able to send a few hundred men there to-morrow, and request, if convenient, that a couple of gun-boats be detailed to accompany them. Will you please inform me if this can be done?*[26]

Dahlgren replied the next day:

> *I am able to inform you that with a view to some communication with General Sherman I had already placed two gun-boats inside the harbor of Georgetown, and have ordered other vessels there, to be in readiness for any movement that might be of use to General Sherman. The Santee has but little depth at its bar, and I am therefore obliged to send such vessels as can enter. The* Geranium, *a tug of about six or seven feet draft, was sent there, with two howitzer launches, to pioneer the way for the* McDonough, *and to examine the channel as well as the road to Georgetown. I just learned that the* Geranium *finds it too rough, and is now at Georgetown awaiting an opportunity to get into the Santee, but she will no doubt obey the orders soon as it is possible to do so. Am I to understand that the gun-boats are to accompany the troops from this place to Georgetown or after they reach that place? Orders for either will be given if you will please to let me know what you desire.*[27]

Georgetown fell to the Federals on February 24, when a small U.S. Navy squadron entered the harbor and discovered that the Confederate batteries that had been guarding the bay were abandoned. Union military leaders quickly set up a base of operations in that city. "It would be very well to keep a dispatch boat at Georgetown, with orders to report without delay," wrote General J.D. Webster to General Gilmore on February 28. Federal military leaders also viewed Georgetown as a possible destination for Sherman, should his march through the South Carolina interior run into trouble. "We do not think it very likely that General Sherman will communicate through Georgetown; but as he distinctly directed a lookout to be kept for him there we wish not to lose any of the chances," Webster told Gilmore. Seven marine companies and a fifteen-gun battery were assigned to garrison the town.[28]

Admiral Dahlgren described Georgetown as having about two hundred residents. Captain Luis F. Emilio of the 54th Massachusetts Regiment described

Georgetown as having "decayed wharves, regular streets, some fine residences, public buildings, and the hall of the Winyaw [*sic*] Indigo Society."[29]

Corporal Albert Rowe Barlow of the 157th New York recalled:

> *Duty at* [Georgetown] *was outpost and town-guard duty. It was a picnic for the boys of Co. G. They cleaned-up, shone, worked very little and grew in fatness. With the easy soldiering a plentiful spicing of fun was always on foot.*
>
> *When off duty considerable liberty was given the men. Occasionally some contraband who had offended in a slight degree was mercilessly seized and tossed on a blanket: At night the strains of Ziba's violin were heard, and when balls were given the colored people gathered at a vacant warehouse and hoed-it-down finely, their bare feet slapping the boards like shutters loose in the wind. And occasionally one of the soldiers was seen stepping out with a colored lass and dancing the hours away. Those balls were very high-toned.*[30]

Poor weather had delayed Sherman's instructions from reaching Gilmore, but on March 27, Gilmore told Brigadier General John Porter Hatch in Charleston:

> *Brigadier-General Potter has been directed verbally to report to you to talk of the expedition to Sumterville and Florence. Rendezvous the command with as little delay and as quietly as possible at Georgetown. Its strength and composition is to be as follows: Two thousand five hundred infantry, one section of artillery, fifty cavalry (or more, if you can spare them), sixty to seventy engineers. The men should carry forty rounds of ammunition in their cartridge-boxes and three days' rations of hard bread, sugar, and coffee in their haversacks, with a reserve of forty or fifty rounds of ammunition and eight days' rations of bread, sugar, and coffee on pack animals. One hundred and fifty pack-saddles are sent you. I want no wagons with the command if it can be avoided.*
>
> *The only tools which the engineers will require are axes, shovels, and augurs, and these the men must carry. It would be well to issue an axe and a shovel to each infantry company. General Potter and myself have talked the matter over pretty thoroughly, and he is in possession of my views.*
>
> *The medical director has been directed to send five or six ambulances with the command, and to designate a suitable medical officer to go with it as senior.*

Brigadier General John Porter Hatch, commander, U.S. Military District of Charleston, is shown seated and surrounded by his staff in this 1865 photo taken in Charleston, South Carolina. The veteran officer was initially ordered to supply Potter's men and later ordered to send troops from Charleston to support the raiders. *Courtesy of the Library of Congress.*

> *Dispatch is quite necessary in the preparations. I expect to be at Georgetown on Friday morning.*[31]

That same day, Gilmore told Dahlgren:

> *General Hatch, commanding at Charleston, informed me on the 20th instant that he had requested your assistance in examining the Santee River and some of the streams flowing into Winyah Bay with a view to the selection of the best route for an expedition to reach Sumterville and Florence, S.C.*

> *Brigadier-General Potter will command the expedition, and I respectfully request for him such co-operation as you may be willing and able to afford. General Potter has been directed to confer with you upon this matter.*[32]

However, Dahlgren was not able to provide much assistance. "You are probably aware that the bar of the Santee prevents the entrance of any but the lightest draft tugs of the squadron," Dahlgren responded on April 1. "My ability, therefore, will be very limited, but such vessels as are suitable will be sent into the river. These will be one or two tugs and some launches carrying howitzers."[33]

On March 29, Gilmore forwarded Sherman's letter to Brigadier General John Rawlins, chief of staff of the United States Armies:

> *The expedition is to start from Georgetown, and would have been off before now if a heavy northeaster, which is still raging, had not delayed the concentration of the troops. It will probably start day after to-morrow for Florence, and will then move on Sumterville, returning by way of the shortest route to transports on Santee River. I most heartily approve and shall cordially carry out in good faith the views of General Sherman and the orders of the lieutenant-general in regard to the reduction to the minimum of the garrisons on this coast. Between 800 and 900 of the 5,000 white troops which I ordered to go to North Carolina I shall detain until the expedition returns.*[34]

The man chosen to lead the expedition was Edward Elmer Potter. Born on June 21, 1823, in New York City, he was a graduate of Columbia University and a trained lawyer. Potter spent much of his prewar career farming. In 1862, he was commissioned as a captain in the commissary department and accompanied Major General Ambrose Burnside's North Carolina Expedition. Although just a commissary officer, Potter was told by Burnside to recruit among the local Unionists to organize the 1st North Carolina (Federal) Infantry.[35] Despite a lack of formal military training, Potter was made the regiment's lieutenant colonel and was later promoted to brigadier general. He spent most of the next two years as Major General John G. Foster's chief of staff. In 1864, he was sent to Charleston, where he took part in many of the operations to take the city, again under General Foster. He was also active in the capture of Georgetown.[36]

Potter would command a "provisional division" of 2,500 to 2,700 men organized into two brigades on the expedition into the Palmetto State. The first

Brigadier General Edward E. Potter, commander, Provisional Division, U.S. Army. Despite a lack of formal military training and experience, Potter proved to be an exceptional field commander. *Courtesy of the Walker Local History and Family History Center, Richland Library, Columbia, South Carolina.*

troops to arrive were the 54th Massachusetts Colored Infantry, which reached Georgetown on March 31. Most of the rest were in Georgetown by April 2.[37]

The most experienced troops were in the First Brigade, led by Colonel Phillip P. Brown Jr., commander of the 157th New York Volunteers. Brown was born in New York State in 1823. A graduate of Madison University (modern-day Colgate University in Hamilton, New York), he was a school principal when the war started. In 1862, he entered the army as a colonel in the 157th New York. He and his men had seen action at the Battles of Chancellorsville and Gettysburg. Afterward, they were transferred to the Department of the South and took part in the numerous operations around Charleston for the next year and a half, save for a few months spent performing garrison duty at Fort Pulaski in Savannah, Georgia.[38]

The rest of Brown's brigade consisted of the 56th New York, the 25th Ohio and the 107th Ohio. All three infantry regiments had once been a part of the XI Federal Army Corps of the Army of the Potomac and had seen action at the Battles of Second Manassas, Chancellorsville and Gettysburg. In August 1863, the corps was sent to South Carolina, where it participated in siege operations around Charleston.[39]

Commanding the Second Brigade was Colonel Edward Needles Hallowell, commander of the 54th Massachusetts. He was born in Philadelphia in 1837 to a Quaker family with strong abolitionist beliefs. When the war began, he was a merchant in Medford, Massachusetts. Hallowell enlisted as a second lieutenant with the 22nd Massachusetts in January 1862 and saw action in the Peninsula Campaign and the Battles of Antietam and Fredericksburg. In March 1863, Hallowell transferred to the 54th Massachusetts as a captain. His brother Norwood, who was originally the lieutenant colonel of the regiment, had been given command of the all-black 55th Massachusetts

The 54th Massachusetts Infantry Regiment. This Currier & Ives print depicts the regiment's historic charge against Battery Wagner in 1863. The scene was re-created in the 1989 Academy Award–winning film *Glory*. *Courtesy of the National Archives.*

Infantry. Consequently, Edward Hallowell was promoted to major in April 1863 and then lieutenant colonel in May, when he assumed the position as second in command of the regiment under Colonel Robert Shaw.[40]

Hallowell was wounded three times during the attack on Battery Wagner outside Charleston on July 18, 1863. He was sent home to Massachusetts to recover. After he recovered, he was promoted to colonel and returned to command the 54th Massachusetts in September 1863. After the Battle of Olustee (Florida), he and the 54th returned to the Charleston area, where they took part in the sieges of Fort Fisher and Charleston.[41]

His brigade included the 32nd U.S. Colored Regiment, five companies of the 102nd U.S. Colored Troops, four companies of the 1st New York Engineers, the Second Battalion of the 4th Massachusetts Cavalry and Battery B of the 3rd New York Artillery. Because of the presence of the all-black regiments, the Second Brigade was sometimes referred to as the "Colored Brigade." However, like all black regiments of its day, its officer corps was all white.[42]

The 32nd Colored had been organized in Philadelphia in 1864 and had been a part of the siege of Charleston. The 102nd Colored had originally been a part of the 1st Michigan Colored Infantry Volunteers, who had seen action in Florida and in the Charleston siege operations. The 1st New York Engineers had been organized in New York City in 1861 and had participated in the capture of Beaufort and the surrounding area in 1862. The regiment was broken up in the spring of 1864 when eight companies were sent to Virginia while four stayed in South Carolina. Those four participated in operations around Charleston.[43]

The only cavalry unit in the expedition, the 4th Massachusetts, had been founded in 1864. Its Second Battalion had seen action in Florida and along the South Carolina coast. Battery B of the 3rd New York Artillery was formed in 1861 in New York City. Originally an infantry unit, it was changed to a light artillery battery in 1862. As a part of the XVIII Federal Army Corps, it had seen action in North Carolina and Virginia. It was sent to South Carolina in January 1863 and stayed in the Palmetto State for the remainder of the war. It marched with "one section of 12-pounder Napoleons, 37 men, 28 horses, 360 rounds of ammunition."[44]

The makeup of this "provisional division" suggests that it was hastily put together using what units were available at the time. The fact that it was led by a brigadier general as opposed to a major general, the usual rank of divisional commanders, substantiates this theory. Also, the presence of black regiments, who, due to racial prejudice, were usually not put into combat situations, further lends credence to this idea.[45]

Chapter 2

The Raid Begins

Potter arrived in Georgetown on April 1, 1865, and took command of his forces. The next day, while General Robert E. Lee's Army of Northern Virginia was evacuating Richmond, Virginia, Potter's men staged a review for Gilmore in "a large ploughed field." Two days later, Gilmore gave Potter his final instructions, and at 8:00 a.m. on April 5, the Federal raiders left Georgetown. The plans for the raid might have been held in strict secrecy, as one officer wrote in his diary on the morning the raid started that he "heard we were to start on a raid this morning."[46]

The original plan was for Potter's men to be carried as far inland as possible by naval transports, but this plan was abandoned when the navy could not provide the needed vessels. Gilmore told Hatch, "[Potter] will strike the Santee River somewhere above the railroad bridge, and has made arrangements to meet his light-draft transports, with extra rations, &c., there…with orders to make all the display possible; clear the bank of the Santee above the railroad bridge of guerrillas." In addition, the armed transport *Savannah* and the transports *Hooker* and *Planter*, with rations and ammunition, were ordered up the Santee River to Murray's Ferry to await orders from Potter. A small naval force of tugs and launches was also ordered to report to the rendezvous site.[47]

Gilmore also ordered that Brigadier General Alfred S. Hartwell, "after he opens communication with General Potter on the Santee River, shall remain there until he hears the result of General Potter's operations at the front, so as to be in position to help General Potter if he is forced back to the river."[48]

Georgetown, South Carolina. This historic port city was the starting point for the raid. *Photo by the author.*

Hatch was ordered to "keep General Potter supplied with rations, seeing that he uses them very frugally and lives as far as possible on the country. You will, if possible, use the steamer *Houghton* for this purpose. General Hartwell must not wait until General Potter is annihilated; but if General Potter needs and call for the men of General Hartwell's command they must go across the Santee and help him."[49]

Gilmore wrote to Sherman on April 9, "The expedition which you ordered is…now well on its way. Its starting was delayed some days by a number of coincident causes…It goes to Sumterville first, and I expect a good account of it. You may hear from it sooner than I do."[50]

Led by the first brigade, the raiders left Georgetown on the Sampit road for three miles, marching on the south side of the road along the Black River before turning right toward Kingstree. Marching through heavily timbered country with no enemy in sight, they traveled nineteen miles and camped for the night near Johnson's Swamp. The first day's march had not been pleasant. "The feet of the men were wet nearly all day," wrote Corporal Barlow, "and wet feet meant blisters."[51]

The next day was warm and humid, which led to exhaustion and straggling among the men. Potter would describe the country his men marched through the first two days as "poor and sandy." Lieutenant Edward L. Stevens of the 54th Massachusetts noted in his diary, "The country we passed through is the most desolate imaginable. We passed but two or three houses all day & those of the meanest kind." Major Edward C. Culp of the 25th Ohio would later write, "Our march had been through an almost unbroken wilderness of pines, and the country did not have a promising look for forage." As they neared Kingstree, the country improved, and the raiders were able to find forage for their animals, as well as hams and sweet potatoes. The one drawback was that it rained hard as the men reached camp.[52]

Meanwhile, the movements of Potter's men did not go unnoticed by what was left of the Confederate government in South Carolina. The state's governor, Andrew Magrath, had fled Columbia just prior to Sherman's capture of the city on February 17, 1865. Since then, he had been traveling across the upper part of the state. Further hampering the governor's efforts to restore the state's government was the fact that much of the state's infrastructure, most notably telegraph lines, river bridges and railroad lines, had been destroyed by Sherman.[53]

Still, Magrath could not sit back and do nothing. Rumors were flying that Potter was marching with fifteen to twenty thousand men, ten times his actual numbers. On April 4, the

Governor Andrew Gordon Magrath. Although the South Carolina governor recognized the danger his state was facing, he had too few men and resources to deal with the crisis. *Author's collection.*

governor ordered out the state militia—in particular Colonel George W. Lee's 20th South Carolina Militia, which consisted entirely of men from the Sumter District—to assemble in Sumter. The men from the Georgetown area were to gather at the home of Colonel James F. Pressley, who was recovering from battle wounds.[54]

To say that Magrath was "scrapping the bottom of the barrel" is an understatement, as most of the militia consisted of men who were too old, too young or unfit for regular army service. Decades after the war, Private James Graves Ramsey recalled, "Every man was an enrolling officer, and a uniformed man was at a premium. The hospitals were stripped of convalescents, sick and wounded soldiers at home on honorable furlough. The stores were cleared of old men and boys, and every man was handed a sorry musket with inferior ammunition."[55]

However, Colonel Pressley was able to gather 1,600 Confederates to make a stand at Lower Bridge over the Black River. Dr. Samuel D. McGill recalled, "Every man capable of bearing arms was in our little army." They effectively tore up all the area bridges, most notably Seven-Mile Bridge.[56]

Mrs. E.A. Steele of Black Mingo, South Carolina, would write:

> *To-day we have heard that a detachment of Potter's raiders are between here and Georgetown, only a few miles from Black River, and making directly for Brown's Ferry. The "home band," an impromptu cavalry made up of young men, boys and old men, have gone down there to intercept them. They will destroy the bridges and flats, thus causing the blue-coats to take a much longer march in reaching us. Here, in this little corner of Williamsburg, with the wide waters of Black River between us and that fire-fiend band, we can hide in safety for a few more days.*
>
> *News has come back to us that our boys reached the ferry, destroyed the flat and gave Potter's men a few short pointed salutes from their muskets, causing them to file on up the river carrying two wounded comrades with them. The crossings at Potato Ferry and the lower bridge were destroyed in turn, and the blue-coats kept on the other side of the river, our little band keeping even pace with them and occasionally making a target of some stray fellow that had loitered behind in a greedy search for plunder.*[57]

Instead of challenging the Confederates, Potter's men moved on, camping for the night at Thorntree Swamp, about seven miles outside of Kingstree. However, that was not enough for Mrs. Steele and her female companions:

> *Secure as we let ourselves to be, there was a universal belief that the Yankees would be amongst us in a short time…consequently there was grave questioning as to what would be done in case they did come. Aunts Carrie and Eleanor, with some half dozen friends, were to meet at our house on the following Tuesday evening to discuss the important subject. Mother and aunts had decided that a place known as "THE DEVIL'B DINING-ROOM" was the best place for concealment in the neighborhood, so good indeed that it was doubtful if anyone could get into it at all. It was a dense growth of lowland, composed of briar and a mixture of low and high shrubbery that grew in such tangled and close confusion it was impossible for the rays of the sun to penetrate it. Inside this green wall was an island-like opening, smooth, high and dry, and which was accessible only by a narrow hog path, which ran through the close, outer wall of briars close to the ground. Any human being entering this wild acreage would have to crawl on hands and knees.*
>
> *Fancy for a moment a frightened bevy of young ladies filing in solemn order through that dark archway in the manner represented above! But ridiculous as the in-going would be, once inside there was safety for themselves.*[58]

Mrs. Steele continued:

> *The details of the arrangement were all settled very soon, indeed there was not much to settle. Each member of the fugitive band was to take with her only such articles as she could not part with at any cost. Two old trusty negroes, a man and woman belonging to grandmother, were to be taken along to cook, for of course they expected to stay there several days. Then there was a box of provisions to be taken by each one. Of course the boxes must need be small, else they could not be dragged through the hog path. Then there were the comforts for the camp bed, one to each individual, and a cup and saucer, a coffee pot and an oven. At last the list of necessities ran so high it was feared the "dining-room" would not accommodate them all and there was a general hubbub as to which articles could be left.*[59]

As they were making the final preparations for this task, a friend of theirs came in and told the ladies, "Potter has rounded us and we won't have to go to the 'dining-room' at all."[60]

On the morning of the seventh, Potter had Major Francis F. Webster take his 4th Massachusetts cavalry to Murray's Ferry "with orders for the transports to ascend the Santee to the Camden railroad bridge, or as near that point as possible."[61]

Potter reported to Gilmore:

> *I reached this point last night. The enemy yesterday destroyed the bridge over the Black River at this point, to prevent our advance to Kingstree. Another bridge is burning beyond, probably the railroad bridge. A few guerrillas have been in our front. I shall make for the place last mentioned in our conversation, where I have reason to think the object can be accomplished. I send the cavalry this morning to Murray's Ferry to order the boats farther up and will communicate with them afterward. We have destroyed considerable cotton and rosin, and are beginning to get horses and mules.*[62]

Captain Luis F. Emilio of the 54th Massachusetts recalled that they marched toward the northwest in "a more open and settled country, containing more abundant supplies which our foragers secured," though the Federals burned all the cotton and mills in their path.[63]

The 54th Massachusetts found themselves in some light skirmishing with Confederates. Nonetheless, the raiders were able to reach the Northeastern Railroad that day and "broke the track for several miles" and destroyed Eppes' Bridge on the Black River. Lieutenant Stevens would call the area "the meanest place I ever saw, black water & black mud." Meanwhile, the 102nd Colored Troops destroyed the Kingstree Bridge over the same stream.[64]

The Reverend William W. Mood of Milford, South Carolina, had gone to Bishopville on April 4 and was dismayed to learn that it would be impossible for the Confederate army in North Carolina, under the command of General Joseph Johnston, to stop Sherman. He and his companions started back to Manning on the sixth, but the reverend fell ill on the trip and stopped at the Mount Zion Presbyterian Church to rest. Though Reverend Mood's companions disagreed, the minister insisted that they continue back to Manning, and after a brief rest, they resumed their journey.[65]

About five or six miles outside Manning, they came upon a hard-riding Confederate soldier, who one of the reverend's companions knew. "He seemed much excited as in hurried tones he told us that every man was ordered to assemble under arms at Manning," wrote Reverend Mood, "that an army largely composed of negroes was marching from Georgetown, S.C., through Salem, to destroy everything and to prevent more farming operations. That it was an army of destruction." The party made it back to Manning before nightfall, where, after being treated for fever, Reverend Mood was told it would have been better for him to have stayed in Bishopville.[66]

Black River, Williamsburg County, South Carolina. The Confederates' successful destruction of the bridges over this river forced Potter to change the route of the raid. *Photo by the author.*

By now, the raiders' reputation was starting to precede them. Sumter resident Emma Holmes noted that as early as Monday, April 3, there was "rumor of a large body of [Federal] troops, marching on Sumter, then through Clarendon and Stateburg up here, to destroy the immense quantity of rolling stock & commissary stores and ammunition run up on this road for safety."[67]

However, Culp claimed after the war that "all gin mills and cotton in our line of march were destroyed, but no private dwellings were burned." Likewise, Corporal Barlow claimed that the 157th New York provided provost guards to prevent looting.[68]

Reverend Mood heard that the raiders "had been to Mrs. Col. Jas E. Davis', three miles from Manning, had swept her of everything, burning her home and the outbuilding." He added, "They were a crowd of robbers, all of them, officers, marines, negro soldiers, and camp followers." Another person claimed that the "Raiders butchered all the cattle and sheep south of the Black River and left their carcasses to rot in the fields and swamps. They burned all the homes and destroyed all the plantation shade trees."[69]

At dusk on April 7, with the reverend too ill to move, two armed friends came to see Reverend Mood, urging him to flee before it was too late. However, the minister refused, saying he was too ill and that he could not abandon his family. The Confederate evacuation left Reverend Mood as the only white male in the town.[70]

The reverend was pleased to learn that his friends Edwin Ruthern Plowden and Edgar Nelson Plowden, both formerly of the 21st South Carolina Infantry Regiment, had burned the bridge over Brewington Swamp under orders from the governor, in the hopes it would slow or detour the raiders.[71]

On the morning of April 8, Potter's men discovered Plowden's handiwork. Since it would have taken a whole day to replace the 120-foot-long span, Potter decided to move toward Manning, which was ten miles farther west.[72]

The 54th Massachusetts found itself marching eighteen miles that day "over fair roads through a wooded country, with a bright sky overhead." They saw the few Confederate defenders "now and then on the flanks and front." They entered the town at dusk.[73]

On the other hand, the army was now joined by seven to eight hundred escaped slaves of all ages and both sexes. Lieutenant Stevens colorfully noted of the group:

> *Almost all the little children carry a tub or something on their heads. The women are the greatest sights, some of them are very pert pretty damsels, of all colors. Some attractive old women just alive. Some young women are like brutes almost*

> *with bosoms as large as a cow's bag hanging down. Most of them have a child in arms, a child at the back & a child about to appear. Such a sight for an artist it is to see these poor people just liberated, going on happy, under such burdens as they bear, keeping up with veteran soldiers in the long wearisome marching. It is sad & yet encouraging to see the hope in their countenances & their perfect trust in us. What is to become of this Race of uneducated, hopeful, anxious people*[?] *What a change has the war bro*[ugh]*t about.*[74]

During the march, Potter and eight members of his staff stopped at the home of John Belton Bagnal, located near the New Zion Methodist Church, for lunch. Though the meal was prepared from their own rations by Potter's own cook, "every chicken, goose, turkey and duck was taken from the family."[75] While the general enjoyed his meal, it rained, causing Potter to order his men to clean out their guns and reload and fire. Allegedly, the target of their aim was the church, which was burned after they left.[76]

Upon arriving in Manning after dark, Potter's cavalry drove a small group of teenage Confederate scouts, sent by Governor Magrath to assess the

Manning, South Carolina. This was the first town occupied by the raiders on April 8, 1865. *Photo by the author.*

situation, out of the town, but not before the scouts burned "a causeway, a mile in length, with six bridges, here crossed the Pocotaligo River and swamp." However, the bridges "were not entirely destroyed."[77]

The Confederate scouts, who were feeding their horses, had just sat down to enjoy a meal for themselves when a lady screamed, "The Yankees are in the street!" The Confederates quickly mounted their horses amidst "a pandemonium of yells and oaths and charging steeds."[78]

One Confederate officer was killed when he refused to surrender. Another Confederate, William Brunson, escaped capture by running through a house and out the backyard. He made it to the swamp, where he hid out until able to safely make his way back to his home in Florence.[79]

The leader of the scouts, Lieutenant Charles Jones of the 7th South Carolina Cavalry, had to shoot his way to freedom. As Federals called out for him to surrender, Jones replied, "I'll show you how to surrender" and then shot and killed Private Charles H. Pratt of the 4th Massachusetts Cavalry in the process. The Union cavalryman was buried in an unmarked grave behind a house on Brooks Street, where his body is said to be still buried.[80]

Jones rode through the streets on the dead Federal's horse while firing his gun at the Union soldiers, who were raining bullets on him as they pursued him. He eventually stopped by a creek and raised his empty gun in a defiant, if not dangerous, attempt to get the Federals to chase him. However, the Federals chose not to give chase. All the while, the men under his command escaped safely. Jones ran into the swamps. He scouted the town that night and, finding that Potter's men were still present, went on to Sumter.[81]

That night, Potter had Hallowell's brigade cross the swamp and river "on the stringers which remained of the bridges." Afterward, "the bridges themselves were rebuilt under the direction of Major Place, First New York Volunteer Engineers." The work was done by midnight.[82]

Major Culp described Manning as "a very pretty place" that "contained some handsome public buildings." Back in Manning, the few hundred local townspeople were living in terror as rumors were swirling that the Federal forces were going to burn the entire town to the ground. The presence of black troops in the town, in which nearly all the houses were lined up one a one-mile-long street, only added to their fears.[83]

Some officers of the 25th Ohio took control of the local newspaper, the *Clarendon Banner*. They printed out a new edition dated Sunday, April 9, 1865, under the title of the *Clarendon Banner of Freedom*.[84] "It may be expected of us to appear very humble in invading this sanctum; whence has issued so many articles of the straightest Secession orthodox, but for our part we 'can't see it,'" ran the lead article in the paper. It went on to say, "We understand that our general does not intend to burn the town, but if we have our way, this office shall no more poison the political atmosphere of the country with its foul odors. The newspapers of the South have done more towards bringing about the Rebellion than aught else, and they should not be spared."[85]

The paper also ran and advertisement for "800 able bodied American citizens of African descent for soldiers in the U. States army. Three hundred dollars bounty will be paid, together with rations, clothing and monthly pay the same as white soldiers. Address: U.S. Recruiting Officer, Georgetown, S.C."[86]

Reverend Mood's house was occupied by black troops. The minister was interrogated by Union army officers, one of whom, a Lieutenant Waterman, told him point blank, "You should have not remained here." To make a bad situation worse, someone had told Potter that Reverend Mood had shot a Union soldier. "The entire army are [*sic*] angered, and the consequences is the town is to be destroyed, anyway, this house is to be burned, they are determined on it."[87] When the reverend protested that he was too ill to have done the deed, Waterman told him, "I know from the inquiries I have made in the town that it could not have been you, but mad and enraged as they are, they will have it that it is you, and they swear vengeance. You'll be made a prisoner and you must dress and prepare for the worse [*sic*]."[88]

Though he was very ill, Reverend Mood was told he would have to walk, as the Federals' wagons were "few and loaded." This led the minister to quip, "Then I'll not walk far." The lieutenant advised Mood, "Don't resist them in any way. Do as they tell you, and be quiet." He was also told not to take anything of value and to hide any important papers in his boots.[89]

After the sun went down, some Michigan soldiers politely asked Mrs. Mood for a towel. She was visibly surprised when they graciously returned it to her. This amused the troops, one of whom told her, "You thought we were thieves and wouldn't return the towel. We are from Michigan and won't rob you." To which the lady replied, "I thought it was such an old affair, I thought it not worth returning." The soldiers thanked her and said, "Lady, we'll not rob you, but we can't say the same for all the men, and if you don't get a guard, you'll have stolen from you all you have before night. You can get a guard for the asking."[90]

They pointed her to Potter's headquarters, located in the house of Dr. H.H. Huggins, and told her that the general was "a kind-hearted man." She told her husband this information, and with a servant, she went to the general's headquarters. He politely greeted her and listened to her request. After confirming her tale with several others in the house, he granted her request for a guard.[91]

The mother of a Mrs. M.R.R. also asked for and received a guard, a Major Campbell, who was described as a "gentlemen" who treated the women of the house "with the greatest kindness and courtesy." They were lucky, as Potter's men were destroying the town, burning the courthouse, jail, stores and warehouses. Mrs. M.R.R. claimed that "cruel, heartless deeds" were perpetrated by the soldiers, including some harsh treatment of some elderly women. One resident would later write that Potter's men "left [Manning] in ashes—a heap of smoking, smoldering ruins." However, Lieutenant Stevens claimed that he had not "heard of any act of wanton conduct on the part of any man in my command."[92]

Potter's men stayed in Manning overnight and left on Sunday morning, April 9, the same day that General Robert E. Lee surrendered the Confederate Army of Northern Virginia to Union commander Lieutenant General Ulysses S. Grant. Following the raiders was a band of escaped slaves said to have been from the sea islands of South Carolina and from the areas Potter had come through, with the latter said to have been persuaded by Potter's men to leave their plantation. One witness claimed that the number of these escaped slaves was in the thousands. Lieutenant Stevens put the number at 1,000 to 1,500, while Captain Emilio placed the number in the hundreds.[93]

Lieutenant Stevens noted in his diary that he marched that day through a rich plantation area and found provisions and forage. "We must have burned over half a million dollars' worth of cotton today," he wrote. He also noticed that "not an able bodied man was seen, all the White & blacks have gone to Sumter," and the women and children had "terrible woebegone expressions."[94]

Chapter 3

The Battle of Dingle's Mill and the Occupation of Sumter and Camden

Potter's 2nd Brigade broke camp at 1:30 a.m. on April 9. That morning, soldiers who chewed it received a ration of plugged tobacco that had been "confiscated." The brigade crossed the Pocotaligo Bridge and then marched two miles before camping for the night "in readiness for an attack."[95]

As Potter was leaving Manning, Confederate military officials in Sumter, about twenty miles away, learned of his presence. Immediately, the Confederates sent scouts to Manning to investigate.[96] However, when the scouts got there, they learned that "the whole force crossed [the Black River] on the morning of the 9th." One Confederate later wrote that when they learned that Potter was going to Manning, "we knew that he would go through Sumter." At the time, Sumter was being used as a supply depot, and the local Presbyterian church had been turned into a hospital. Quickly sensing the potential danger to Sumter, the scouts fled back there.[97]

Lieutenant Charles H. Jones passed the information on to Brigadier General Joseph H. Lewis, commander of the 1st Kentucky Brigade, more commonly known as the "Orphan Brigade," which was on the outskirts of Sumter. Lewis was born in 1824. A graduate of Centre College, he had practiced law before the war and was a three-time state legislator who, despite being a Whig Party member, sided with the Confederacy. He had seen action at the Battles of Shiloh, Murfreesboro and Chickamauga. He assumed command of the brigade in 1863.[98]

Lewis started laying out his forces in an attempt to stop or delay Potter. Lieutenant Jones felt that Lewis had too few men to make such a stand and

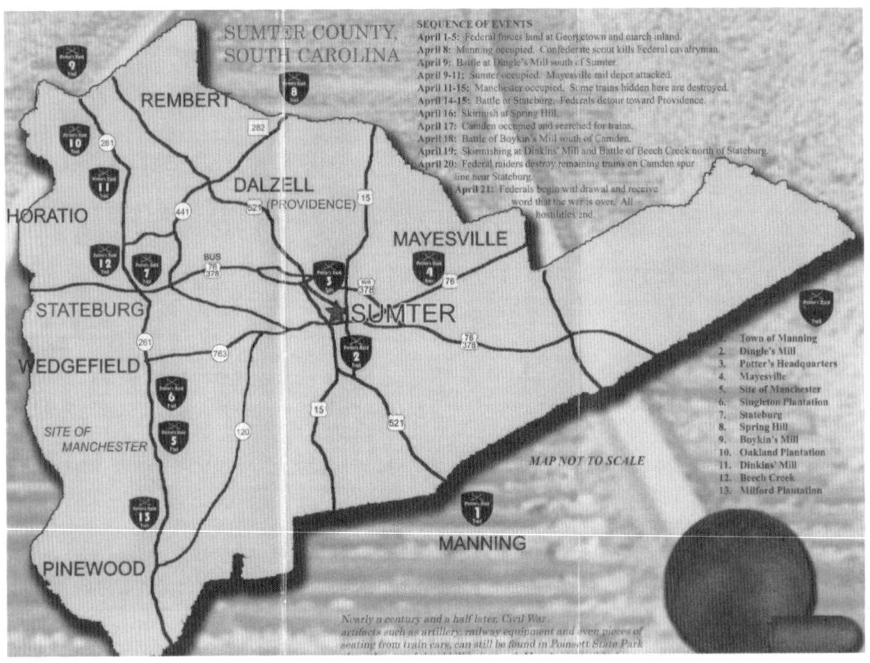

Above: Map of Potter's route in Sumter County, South Carolina, created by local historian Robert Brown and produced by the Sumter County Historical Commission and the Sumter Convention and Visitors' Bureau. *Author's collection.*

Left: Brigadier General Joseph H. Lewis, commander, 1st Kentucky Brigade (aka the "Orphan Brigade"). As one of the most experienced Confederate commanders left in South Carolina, it was Lewis who decided that the Confederates should make a stand at Dingle's Mill. Though the remains of his unit participated in the battle, he withdrew in a snit. *Courtesy of the Library of Congress.*

urged him to concentrate his men at Dingle's Mill, south of Sumter. Lewis did not take kindly to this advice and rather coldly told Jones, "Well sir, you had better take command and I'll retire."[99]

Colonel Thomas Conner, who was in charge of the Clarendon County militia, which by now was reduced to forty men—"hardly a 'corporal's guard'"—made the decision that Manning would have to be left to its fate. He then led his men on an overnight march to Sumter in the hopes that others would gather there to make a stand.[100] When Conner reached Sumter, he was joined by about seven other small militia units that brought total Confederate manpower up to as many as 575. Colonel John W. Caldwell of the 9th Kentucky Mounted Regiment was placed in overall command by virtue of seniority.[101]

Unfortunately, neither Caldwell nor any other Confederate leader had accurate intelligence regarding the size of Potter's forces, how fast they were moving or which roads they were taking. Also hurting their efforts to make a successful defense was the lack of sufficient armaments for the men, as well as the fact that they had only three pieces of artillery.[102] At least sixty-five of the men were wounded Confederate soldiers convalescing at the hospital. Two of the patients, Lieutenant William McQueen, the son of the local Presbyterian minister, and Lieutenant Raphael Painpare of New Orleans, organized the patients into artillery batteries for the two brass howitzers and one iron cannon that had been found.[103]

The makeshift Confederate force left Sumter, without music or fanfare, for Manning, marching through three miles of deep sand until they came to Dingle's Mill, located south of Sumter. Here, crossing the road was Turkey Creek, which had been dammed to form a large millpond that was too deep and murky to cross. One witness described the swamp as "wide, dense, and boggy," adding that "it would not float a blanket, it was so soft." There were only two ways to cross it: by a bridge, which the Confederates had already burned, or across a two-hundred-foot causeway surrounded by woods.[104]

According to Confederate artillerist W.H. Garland, the defenders were on land that was "low and flat, an open field without any natural protection for us; but on the side that General Potter occupied the bank of the stream rose up to quite a hill, and the bank and hill were covered with large oak trees. This gave the enemy a great advantage." To try to even the odds, the Confederates erected two breastworks—one in the middle of the road where McQueen's battery stood and another on the edge of the field—but these efforts "only protected our legs." Garland stood with Painpare's battery, where he held the vent or thin tube at the rear of the gun. It was the only task he could perform, having lost his left hand the year before at City Point, Virginia.[105]

To the Confederates' right stood a building a few yards away from where the mill's wastewater spilled into a thicket. Lieutenant McQueen was in charge of one gun, while Lieutenant Painpare commanded the second. The third gun, the iron one, was commanded by a Sergeant Dunbar, but it would not work due to improper primers. The small battery was masked with pine tops and saplings. Pickets were posted on the left side of the road to watch for Potter's approach. Unfortunately for the Confederate artillerists, the ammunition was not suited for the caliber of the guns.[106]

Despite the potential danger they were facing, the Confederates did not seem too concerned. While they were waiting, they enjoyed a nice meal prepared by the ladies of Sumter, leading one defender to quip, "If we must die, die with a full stomach." Lieutenant McQueen was seen sitting on a gun carriage and laughing with his men.[107]

The people of Sumter were not happy with this defense. Captain Robert Andrews, a veterinary officer in the Confederate army, claimed that the local population tried to "persuade them not to attempt a defense, for they could see that it would exasperate the foe, and lead them on to sack and burn, and this proved to be the case." Catherine Louisa McLaurin echoed this view: "This opposition, feeble as it was, only served to infuriate them the more."[108]

Potter was anxious to take Sumter before dusk. According to his intelligence, the Confederates had moved their railroad equipment from Wilmington to Sumter. A mile from Dingle's Mill, he ordered his division to a halt and ordered a reconnaissance. Before arriving at the mill, he "ordered Colonel Hallowell's brigade to turn the enemy's position on the left by taking a plantation road which led to the main road between Dingle's Mill and Sumterville." Around 2:00 p.m., the Federals neared the millpond, and the small Confederate battery opened fire. According to one witness, the initial Confederate artillery shot and killed five Federals and wounded several others. More significantly, "if it had gone a little lower it would have killed General Potter, as it passed just over his head."[109]

As mentioned, the Confederates had already burned a wooden bridge across the millpond to delay or stop Potter. However, they were unable to remove or destroy the bigger pieces of the span. About this time, a mill building burned. Exactly who started the fire that destroyed the mill is a matter of debate, since both sides claimed credit for it, with the Federals saying they did to prevent sharpshooters. Potter, mistakenly interpreting this

Site of the Battle of Dingle's Mill, Sumter, South Carolina. This turn-of-the-twentieth-century postcard is one of the earliest known images of the site of the April 9 battle. The terrain depicted in this image is probably very similar to what Potter's men marched through. *Author's collection.*

This is a modern view of the same scene depicted in the postcard. *Photo by the author.*

as a retreat by the Confederates, ordered Colonel Houghton to bring the 25th Ohio down to the bridge.[110]

The road doubled as the dam for the pond, which left Colonel Cooper concerned that the enemy might be waiting for his 107th Ohio on the other side. He called for volunteers to cross the burning bridge and reconnoiter the road ahead. Privates Henry S. Finkenbiner, Jacob James and Jacob Brobst volunteered for this task.

Years later, Private Finkenbiner recalled:

> *We received orders to accomplish the mission and report as soon as possible. The enemy's battery was masked on a little knoll that commanded the entire road, and as we crossed at a point about ninety yards from the bridge they could plainly see every move we made, while they were hidden from our view. The support of this masked battery lay still nearer the bridge in a thicket on the right side of our advance.*
>
> *We cautiously went forward, passed the burning mill, and, reaching a place where the road makes a turn towards Sumterville, we saw the enemy for the first time. Instead of creeping back and reporting, we took a shot at them and then ran for the bridge.*
>
> *To our great surprise, we then found ourselves between the enemy's battery and their reserve. A shot of grape and canister but twenty yards from this turn was sent to intercept our run, but we were too near and it flew wide of its mark. The next instant the support just in front and to our right opened fire on us. Their second aim was better, or worse for us, for Brobst fell. His cry, "Don't for God's sake let the rebels get me," brought us to a stop in our headlong rush for safety, and we returned to our fallen comrade.*
>
> *By this time they had our range and were shooting uncomfortably close to us. We picked Brobst up and placed him on my rifle between us, thus carrying him in safety over the burning bridge to an ambulance corps in the woods, in the rear of our army.*
>
> *Just then we saw General Houghton come down the narrow road and file out. Knowing the terrible situation he would get into, I hurried to report our discovery to General Porter, and an orderly was sent forward at once to recall the Twenty fifth Ohio, which would certainly have fared badly had they advanced.*[111]

According to Potter, "Our skirmishers were pushed forward to the edge of the pond, which was skirted with dense thickets, shutting out everything from view on either side. Lieutenant Clark's section of Napoleons returned the fire from the enemy's battery."[112]

The Confederate artillerists were having no luck. Having already lost one cannon before the battle began, they lost a second when Lieutenant Painpare's became choked with shot. Then, in the Federal artillery volley, Lieutenant McQueen was killed when a cannon ball went through his body.[113]

At Lieutenant Painpare's cannon, Garland recalled, "I happened to look down the swamp to our right and rear and saw Yankees jumping over the fence into the field a little over a quarter mile from us. There were several hundred in the field forming in line, and they were still coming over the fence." Garland pointed this out to Painpare, who ordered his men to get behind a corner of the breastworks, saying, "As soon as we fire they will pour a volley into us." The artillerists were in the process of firing their cannon when the Federals fired a volley that struck the lieutenant in the head, killing him instantly, though Garland claimed their last shot killed fifteen to twenty Federals. "We were now flanked, vastly outnumbered, and both our officers killed," wrote Garland, "It was useless for us to attempt to continue the fight, so we at once retreated; and as the horses belonging to the guns had run away when the fight began, we had to leave the guns." One veteran called witnessing the deaths of the two artillery officers "the saddest [scene] in my army life." Before the Federal guns were silenced, they fired fifty-five rounds during the battle.[114]

"Learning from a negro that the swamp could be crossed on the enemy's right," Potter "directed Colonel Brown to order Lieutenant-Colonel [James C.] Carmichael, with the One hundred and fifty-seventh New York Volunteers and the detachment of the Fifty-sixth New York Volunteers, to make the attempt. This he succeeded in doing, gained the enemy's rear, charged and routed him, capturing a battle-flag and two guns."[115]

Barlow recalled of the charge, "The distance the boys traveled in that swamp was fully three-fourths of a mile. In places the water was nearly waist-deep, and logs, bogs, broken timber, tangled vines and drooping limbs, made order impossible."[116]

Private James Graves Ramsey, one of the Confederate gunners, recalled, "We abandoned our guns being flanked out of position. The One Hundred and Fifty-seventh New York regiment and part of the Fifty-sixth New York regiment had been sent some distance down the swamp, below the millrace to effect a crossing. They succeeded, while the 107th Ohio and 25th Ohio regiment were still threatening a passage of the dam in front." In fact, the small Confederate forces were facing 2,500 men. One estimate put the Confederate defenders at this point down to 158, giving the Federals a 16–1 advantage.[117]

Meanwhile, Colonel Hallowell's 54th Massachusetts "met a small force of the enemy's cavalry" and came close to capturing fifty men under Colonel George Lee. However, two-thirds of the way into the swamp, the Federals' guide disappeared, resulting in Caldwell being unable to gain the main road. According to Potter, "this prevented the capture of the enemy's whole force." Colonel Hallowell was ordered to rejoin the main column, and the march was resumed toward Sumterville. However, Lee's men escaped singly and not as a whole, so it was impossible for him to regroup them for the rest of Potter's raid.[118]

With his artillery silenced, the 157th and 56th New York turning the Confederate flanks and the militia fleeing from a bayonet charge from the 25th Ohio, Caldwell had no choice but to order a retreat back to Sumter, though the Confederates were exposed to enemy fire for almost a mile past the battle site. Potter described the Confederate retreat as "complete disorder." Potter would also claim that he had fought against "700–800 men, chiefly local troops" listed 26 men as casualties and reported Caldwell's loss as being "larger." One Confederate account placed their casualties at 13 men killed, wounded or captured. Potter also reported the capture of a battle flag and the three pieces of Confederate artillery. Potter did not pursue the retreating Confederates, instead tending to his wounded and burying his dead in a large pit.[119]

After the shooting had died down, Potter rode to the battlefield and complimented Colonel Carmichael and his men for their gallantry. Carmichael in turn presented Potter the captured Confederate guns and colors. The next day, Potter gave the 56th New York the colors and battle honors by virtue of having two companies in the main assault. Although Barlow considered his fellow New Yorkers to be "good soldiers," he felt that giving the 56th New York the honors was "altogether cheeky," especially since the 157th New York had done the hardest fighting, suffered the greatest loss and was first inside the Confederates battery.[120]

Potter would later commend Colonel Henry L. Chipman of the 102nd U.S. Colored Troops for joining the battle "with five companies of his regiment after a march of considerable difficulty, and in the affair at Dingle's Mill rendered excellent service."[121]

Three Federal privates of the 107th Ohio—Henry S. Finkenbiner, Jacob James and Jacob Brobst—were cited by Colonel Brown for their bravery:

> *These three men were on the advanced skirmish line, and while in direct range and close fire of the enemy's artillery, crossed the bridge on the mill-*

These memorial markers honor three Union soldiers whose remains were buried in a common grave somewhere on the battlefield site. *Photo by the author.*

> *race, to ascertain the enemy's position. The danger incurred and daring evidenced by their conduct are such as reflect the highest military credit upon themselves and their regiment. One of them, Jacob Brobst, was wounded, and has since lost his leg. He could not have suffered more gloriously.*
>
> *The Colonel commanding* [the] *brigade returns his thanks to these men: he is sure that their heroism will be a matter of pride, and an object of emulation with his entire command.*[122]

The defeated Confederates rushed back into Sumter. One of the first was Donald McQueen, the younger brother of the slain artillery officer, who galloped into town carrying his dead brother's hat and sash, crying out, "They have killed my brother!"[123]

The women of the town, fearing the worse, immediately secured their doors and windows and hid in their homes. Emma Holmes wrote in her diary, "Everyone was in a state of painful anxiety from uncertainty & dread of the black troops being let loose on us."[124]

Potter's cavalry entered Sumter late in the afternoon of April 9, having marched eighteen miles that day. The 25th Ohio sang "Rally 'Round the Flag" as they entered the town. Potter set up his headquarters at the Solomons' house on Main Street while frightened townswomen went to the Altamont Moses house to obtain guards. Captain Emilio described the town as boasting "good dwellings, two female seminaries, and the usual public buildings." Lieutenant Stevens likewise noted that "Sumter is a beautiful place, stylish people, refined, highly educated."[125]

Allegedly, one of the first things the Federals did was to round up all the blacks in the town. They were then sent to the train depot, where the black troops of Potter's command were camping. In addition, Federal troops, both black and white, went from house to house officially searching for weapons or hidden Confederate soldiers but also taking food, clothing and other valuables in the process.[126]

Soon afterward, fires were reported in the depot, railroad shops and some cotton warehouses. The flames spread to a row of one- and two-room houses where the railroad employees lived. Reportedly, officers found shoes and swords. Lieutenant Stevens himself took a pair of boots; others got china and silverware. A big treat was peanuts found among the Confederate rations left behind. Also found were cigars.[127]

Captain Andrews later complained, "On came the troops; now burning and destroying everything before them, which they would not have been done, had they not been fired upon, and many a stately residence...would otherwise be standing today." His clever wife saved their house by greeting a Federal cavalry officer and offering him refreshments while asking for, and receiving, protection.[128]

Andrews further claimed that the Federals came looking for him, but he avoided capture by hiding near his home and then fleeing Sumter. He hid out in a swamp for a week until he learned that the war was over. Much to his relief, he returned to Sumter to find that his family and most of his property had been unmolested.[129]

One local woman, Fannie McKagen, had a horrifying experience with one looter. After scaring the children by putting the barrel of his rifle in their sleeping nurse's mouth, he asked if any of the men folk of the house had fought in the battle earlier that day. When Mrs. McKagen replied that her husband had fought in the battle, the soldier taunted her by saying, "Yes I saw him. He was lying on his stomach and I stuck my bayonet through him and turned him over."[130] This was too much for the sickly woman to bear. Although she later received word from her husband that he was safe and unharmed, the shock worsened her condition to the point that she died within a week, leaving her daughter Mary to say, "That soldier had as truly killed her as if he had stuck his bayonet though her."[131]

Another woman, Jane Cooper Muldrow Haynseworth, was in her flower garden carrying a pair of shears when she sighted some soldiers. Instead of running, she stood on her porch and defiantly told the soldiers, "I'll shoot the first man that puts his foot on that step." She then clicked her shears, which she was holding behind her back, for added effect. Her bluff worked, and the would-be looters fled.[132]

Catherine McLaurin recalled, "Upon their entry into [Sumter], they indulged in many direful threats, and even exhibited to the horrified eyes of mothers and sisters, the clothes taken from the bodies of our loved dead and stained with their blood. No other acts of barbarity were committed, save the murder of an aged gentleman, in defense of his daughter's honor."[133]

Emma Holmes watched the troops enter Sumter and later wrote, "The Yankees came in splendid order, 14 abreast, singing Methodist hymns…The negro troops came last…The whites encamped in the park, the negroes at the lower end of the town," where few guards were placed.[134]

On the other hand, Potter's men were in "fine spirits at having gained the railroad without serious opposition," wrote Emilio. Adding to their cheer was the news that Richmond and Mobile and Selma, Alabama, had all fallen into Federal hands. Potter ordered a cannon salute from captured Confederate artillery to celebrate the Union's success.[135]

There was one humorous incident recorded by Corporal Barlow:

> *After the fight* [at Dingle's Mill] *was over Col. Carmichael observed a man trying to screen himself behind a fence and one of the boys was stirring the fellow with the butt of his rifle. The colonel tapped the Johnny on the head and asked him what he was doing there.*
>
> *"I am only a poor preacher," he replied. The colonel left him, saying to the boys the fellow was not worth taking.*
>
> *As it happened, the wife of a clergyman invited Col. Carmichael to make her house his headquarters. She stated that her husband was not at home and feared he had been taken prisoner. "I would rather he be killed than be a prisoner in your hands," she said.*
>
> *The Colonel went to Gen. Potter's headquarters and returned without finding the missing husband. But while eating supper the subject was renewed and then the incident which discovered the preacher behind the fence, occurred to the colonel.*

> *"Oh, yes, madam," said he, "I know him. I found him down by the woods. I didn't consider him worth taking."*
>
> *Then the fire flew from the eyes of the offended woman. The more she scolded, the more the colonel was amused. He learned later (the fight occurring on Sunday) that when the alarm was given the people were at church. And this preacher, after invoking assistance from the God of battles, went forth with other home-guards to meet the bad Yankees. The idea was not a bad one if he felt that way, but what could he have found interesting behind the fence? Perhaps he had dropped the thread of his discourse and was searching for his "fifteenthly, my brethren." An entertaining sight it must have been when the godly man reached his home and learned that his valor had preceded him.*[136]

Barlow added that his company "did not believe in killing parsons especially if they were armed with Samson's favorite weapon."[137]

The following day, April 10, Potter's men began a systematic destruction of the town. Potter would report on April 26 that his men "destroyed all the railway buildings and machine shops, 4 locomotives, and 20 cars. The railway track was torn up and trestle-work burned for six miles on either side." But on May 6, he claimed to have "destroyed 4 locomotives, 8 cars, carpenter shops, car and blacksmith shops, machine-shop with the stationary engine, freight depot, and store-houses, together with offices and quarters for the employés [*sic*], and 1,000,000 feet of lumber."[138]

The events in Sumter caught the attention of South Carolina native Brigadier General John Preston, formerly the superintendent of the Confederate Bureau of Conscription. From his home in Columbia, he sent the following message to Confederate secretary of war John C. Breckenridge:

> *A raid burnt Sumterville this morning, moving on Camden and toward Chester and the supply trains. Another approaching from Charleston. No guns near; a crippled colonel, commandant. Can I be of service? I am ready for orders. Troops might be sent from Charlotte to meet the movement on Chester. I can use a few militia here.*[139]

Given the fact that a third of Columbia had been destroyed by Sherman less than two months earlier and that much of the South Carolina's infrastructure was destroyed, it is amazing that General Preston's letter was able to make it out of the state. However, Preston's offer was not considered.

Back in Sumter, Potter sent a dispatch to General Gilmore detailing the Battle of Dingle's Mill and the destruction of equipment in Sumter.[140] In detailing his future plans, Potter wrote:

> *Detachments of infantry have been sent up and down the railroad to burn such small bridges as are near here and any cars that may be on the road. More than 1,000 bales of cotton have been burned along our line of march, and there are several hundred bales here waiting that process. I shall move to Manchester to-morrow to communicate with the transports, procure rations, and send off the wounded and contrabands. My subsequent operations will hang upon information gained there. There are six more locomotives between here and Camden. Trains have been running from Florence to the latter place. On our advance the enemy destroyed all the bridges on the Black River. We crossed the Pocotaligo River, or swamp, at Manning. The swamp is crossed by a causeway a mile in length, with six bridges, all of which the enemy fired, but they were not effectually burned. One brigade was crossed on the string pieces which remained, and Major Place rebuilt the bridges during the night. The roads have been good, and the men have marched excellently, averaging from twelve to eighteen miles a day.*[141]

The Sumter merchants could only stand by helplessly as their businesses were ransacked by the Federals. Lieutenant Stevens noted that "the stores had been entered, safes broken open, stores rifled. The soldiers also found lots of well stock drug stores, which were all looted."[142]

The office of the local newspaper, the *Sumter Watchman*, was used to print another Union paper, the *Sumter Banner of Freedom*, which sarcastically announced the fall of Richmond and Petersburg, Virginia. Ironically, it announced the surrender of Lee to Grant on the very day it happened, though none of Potter's men were aware of this at the time. Afterward, all the machinery was destroyed and the type scrambled.[143]

One resident alleged that the black troops "committed some gross outrages violating a young lady," which supposedly led Potter to claim, "Wherever we go that Massachusetts regiment gives us trouble." On the other hand, the very same troops held a camp meeting that attracted crowds of onlookers. "Tremendous excitement prevailed, as they prayed their cause might prosper & their just freedom be ordained," observed Holmes.[144]

Potter's men left Sumter on April 11. Barlow recalled it being "a terribly hot day," which caused the dust to roll up in clouds.[145] According to one account, they stayed in Sumter for only one day, as they were afraid of a

A contraband train. Reportedly, thousands of slaves followed Potter's men during the raid, creating movement and logistics problems for the raiders. Eventually, Potter had no choice but to send them all to Georgetown via Wright's Bluff. *Author's collection.*

surprise attack from the Confederates. Reportedly, most of the town's slaves followed the army. Miss Holmes noted that "great numbers of servants went off from town really crazy from excitement & the parade, as well as the idea of going to Charleston in carriages." However, the trip was an unpleasant one. "Poor deluded creatures, two or three miles from town, their equipage were destroyed…they were marched on, their road traced by broken wagons, dead animals, bundles, drowned infants (15 being found in one pond, thrown by their mothers from exhaustion) & dead women & children."[146]

Major Culp recalled, "The negroes had flocked to us by the thousands and in all sizes and colors. It became a serious problem how to dispose of them. Our wagon train had also increased in size, and was a sight to behold. Vehicles of all descriptions: wagons, buggies, carriages, coaches, and in fact, everything imaginable that was ever placed on wheels—a most absurd procession, and lengthening for miles on the road." In fact, Culp's regiment was delayed on April 11 due to all the time it took to care for all the escaped slaves.[147]

Upon the raiders' departure, the local citizens ventured from their houses to see how the town had fared. Much to their surprise and relief, the damage was not as bad as they had feared or expected. Two townsmen, Augustus

Mayesville, South Carolina. On April 10, while Potter was in Sumter, units from the Second Brigade went to Mayesville, where they destroyed the depot (located to the left of the road), boxcars and other railroad supplies. *Photo by the author.*

Solomon and A.J. Moses, went to Dingle's Mill to tend to the Confederate dead. However, one man, Robert Bee, was found hanging from the rafters of his attic after having been allegedly tortured and murdered by drunken soldiers who were said to have raped his daughter.[148]

On April 10, Potter had sent Major Webster's cavalry to Manchester, about twelve miles west of Sumter. There, they destroyed "one locomotive and train, the railroad buildings, and some Government stores." They also destroyed a long covered railroad bridge, four cars, two hundred bales of cotton, a gin house and a mill filled with corn. Meanwhile, a detachment of black troops moved toward Mayesville, about ten miles northeast of Sumter, whose depot had been used by the Confederates to store supplies. Though the supplies had been moved by the time the Federals got there, the Union troops destroyed seven railroad cars at the town's depot, as well as a bridge.[149]

Potter himself reached Manchester by nightfall. The town dated back to 1790 as a stagecoach station, later serving as a river port before becoming a major point of the 173-mile-long Wilmington and Manchester Railroad, which connected the Palmetto State's interior with the port of Wilmington,

The now-abandoned town of Manchester was once one of the Palmetto State's most important railroad links and perhaps its wildest town. Potter's men destroyed railroad equipment here on April 11. *Photo by the author.*

North Carolina. At its peak, Manchester was South Carolina's own answer to Sodom and Gomorra, as it was known for "dancing, card playing, horse racing, cock fighting, and contests of skill and strength." On one occasion, local citizens chased a circuit-riding preacher out of the town and nearly rioted over a second one.[150]

Unfortunately, there was no water for the troops at Manchester, so the soldiers were ordered to march a little farther. As they were setting up their camp for the night, orders were given for them to move three miles to the Singleton plantation. By the end of the day, they had marched twenty miles, skirmishing all the way.[151]

Potter set up his headquarters at the Singleton plantation, Midway, so named because it was located between two older plantations. Culp described it as "a fine residence…neat and convenient." It was the home of the widowed Mrs. Waites W. Rees, who had fled the house at the approach of the Federals with her children. However, her aged aunt, Mrs. Bentham, stayed behind and saved the house from burning, thanks in part to the help of a small squad of Confederates. One of them, a soldier named York, was allegedly killed for refusing to take the oath of allegiance to the United States. Some accounts state that York was buried near the road, while others say it was in a corner of the house. For years, local ladies decorated his grave on Memorial Day.[152]

This monument marks the site on which the Singleton Plantation house once stood. *Photo by the author.*

Meanwhile, Potter learned that an old classmate, John N. Frierson, lived nearby at Cherryvale, so he and his staff paid a visit to the Frierson's, where the general and his staff were entertained.[153]

The Singleton home was apparently spared, which is a lot more than could be said for several other area homes. At least two area plantation houses, along with numerous outbuildings, were burned. One local resident wrote, "Our anxiety may be imagined as we sat on the piazza, watching the smoke arising from the burning depots, dwellings, [cotton] gin-houses, barns, cotton, etc." The home that seventy-six-year-old E.S. Campbell shared with her daughter and invalid son was almost burned down but was spared, thanks to pleas of an eighteen-year-old slave girl. Sadly, however, the son, who apparently had trouble understanding orders from a black soldier, was killed.[154]

The main mission of the raid was not ignored. At the Wateree Junction, five miles west of Manchester, the railroad trestle, five train engines, thirteen cars, lumber, the turntable and water tanks were destroyed. Three miles farther west in a swamp, three more locomotives with thirty-five cars said to be containing $300,000 in supplies were also destroyed. Until the 1950s, the remains of the destroyed trains could still be seen.[155]

At Manchester, the 54th Massachusetts was sent six miles down the track to a point near Wateree Junction. There, after dark, Lieutenant Colonel

Hooper discovered cars, water tanks and several locomotives, one of which was ready to move.[156] Though it was not known if any Confederate forces were present, it was clear that the locomotive had to be seized before it transported the rolling stock. Quickly, sharpshooters were set up to cover an advance of twenty men led by Lieutenant Stephen Swails and Sergeant Frank Welch.[157]

The Union band chased away fifteen rail hands, who fled into a nearby swamp. Swails personally led his men and jumped into the locomotive's cab. While waving his hat in triumph, Swails was shot in his right arm by one of his sharpshooters, who mistook him for the train's engineer.[158]

Having secured the target, the Federals found that they had captured five engines and thirteen cars, as well as tanks, a turntable and a large quantity of finished timber. A captured slave told them that there was more rolling stock west of their location. After burning a trestle bridge of the Camden branch of the railroad to prevent any surprise Confederate attacks, a raiding party under the command of Captain Charles Tucker was sent to investigate.[159]

Tucker went three miles and captured three locomotives and thirty-five cars without opposition. Since one of the engines was "steamed up," Tucker decided to transport his men back via rail until they reached the burning trestle, at which point they would hike the rest of the way. "Knowing that any delay would be dangerous, and that life and death hung in the balance, I crowded on all steam, and we crossed the bridge through flame and smoke in safety, but with not a moment to spare, for scarcely had we accomplished the passage when it tottered and fell, a heap of blazing ruins."[160]

Meanwhile, the 107th Ohio came from the direction of Camden and joined the 54th Massachusetts, at which time it was decided to transport the two regiments using two locomotives. Lieutenant Swails, whose arm was in a sling, took charge of the lead train with the assistance of Lieutenant William Whitney. Cars were coupled together, which resulted in two injuries. After destroying the property at the junction, the trains slowly headed toward Manchester, burning the trestle after crossing it.[161]

Because the second train moved so slowly, it was decided to lighten the load by dropping cars. Eventually, only the locomotive containing the wounded remained while the rest of the men walked. Lieutenant Colonel Hooper eventually joined his raiders along the roadside. It was hoped that the men could be transported back to Manchester via rail, but a flue had blown out of Swails's engine, so the train and rolling stock were destroyed. Lost in the fire were some captured military supplies. The estimated value of the destroyed items was $300,000.[162]

The 54th Massachusetts rejoined their brigade around 7:00 a.m. on April 12 at the Singleton plantation, located between Manchester and Pinewood, having marched 25 miles in twenty-four hours while working all night and having only one meal. Stevens estimated that they had marched 125 miles in one week with only one day of rest. Potter had established his headquarters at the plantation.[163]

Potter later wrote, "Upon arriving [in Manchester] the Fifty-fourth Massachusetts Volunteers was sent down the railroad to Wateree Junction, while the One hundred and seventh Ohio marched to Middleton Depot, and thence along the Camden railroad to the same point. Eight locomotives and forty cars were destroyed near the Wateree trestle-work, which is three miles in length. A mile of this was burned, as were also some bridges."[164]

However, Potter now had a problem:

> *As the rations of bread, sugar, and coffee were exhausted on the 12th, I sent the wagons and pack-mules to Wright's Bluff, on the Santee, to obtain additional supplies. The wounded and the contrabands* [slaves], *of whom there were large numbers, were also ordered to the same point, to be embarked on the transports. These trains were under escort of the Thirty-second U.S. Colored Troops. The command remained encamped at Singleton's, three miles from Manchester, until the 15th, awaiting the return of the wagons and pack train. Reconnaissances were made to Stateburg and as far as Claremont Station on the road to Camden. Information was gained that the enemy had been re-enforced by two small brigades of cavalry under Major-General* [Pierce Manning Butler] *Young and was intrenching at Boykin's Mill.*[165]

Potter would wait three days for his rations to arrive.

The escaped slaves, estimated by Stevens to be about 2,500, were escorted a distance of twenty-five miles, at which point women, children and the wounded were put in boats to travel to Georgetown. Two hundred captured muskets were given to the men, who were told to march overland to Georgetown, a distance of eighty to ninety miles.[166]

Watching this procession was Miss McLaurin. According to her, it took several hours to pass her by on a night that was "dark and rainy." It was to her ears "very pitiful…to hear the wailing of the poor little babies and young children, who had become separated from their mothers in the general melee. One wagon, loaded with these helpless little creatures, broke down and was abandoned in Stateburg." She further alleged that, in some cases, mothers simply abandoned their babies by the roadside when they got tired of carrying them. The children on this wagon were "kept and cared for by a kind woman until released by death, or reclaimed by their parents in their return from Georgetown, months after."[167]

Another allegation was that at Wright's Bluff, two flat boats full of women and children were drowned. When a third group refused to board a flat boat, they were fired on by the Federals. The escaped slaves then fled to the woods.[168]

Miss McLaurin also questioned the wisdom of sending people "from the healthy up-country at this season of the year to the malarial swamps of the coast." When she posed this question to a Federal officer, he shrugged and said, "I supposed a great many will die." Sadly, his words might have been prophetic, for supposedly many fell victim to "fever, small pox and other disease," though many others returned to their old homes.[169]

Unbeknownst to Potter at the time was the fact that a Federal force was coming from Charleston, South Carolina, to connect with him. On April 5, Gilmore ordered troops be sent from the port city to the Santee region to try to rendezvous with the raiders. Brigadier General John P. Hatch had trouble executing the order, as Charleston was "nearly stripped of [Federal] troops." He did, however, manage to send Brigadier General Alfred S. Hartwell with the 55th Massachusetts, 54th New York and some artillery, but he could send no cavalry, as Potter already had all the available Union horsemen.[170]

Hatch was not very happy with his orders and rather curtly told Gilmore:

> *The instructions relieving me from any control over General Potter's force and directing me to do everything in my power to aid him are received. General Hartwell has instructions to communicate with General Potter and assist him as far as possible. This place being, however, nearly stripped of troops, I have instructed him not to cross the Santee River unless necessary to save General Potter's command from destruction. I suppose the "authority to call on me for help" does not convey the right to take my troops except in an emergency, and to save his own command.*[171]

Hartwell's orders stated that once he "opens communication with General Potter on the Santee River, [he] shall remain there until he hears the result of General Potter's operations at the front, so as to be in position to help General Potter if he is forced back to the river."

"You will keep General Potter supplied with rations, seeing that he uses them very frugally and lives as far as possible on the country. You will, if possible, use the steamer Houghton for this purpose. General Hartwell must not wait until General Potter is annihilated; but if General Potter needs and calls for the men of General Hartwell's command they must go across the Santee and help him."[172]

Despite Hatch's concern about the lack of manpower garrisoning Charleston, more troops were ordered to meet with Potter. On April 8, Gilmore's chief of staff, Colonel Stewart L. Woodward, told Hatch:

> *I am directed by the major-general commanding to inform you that he has ordered the balance of the One hundred and second U.S. Colored Troops, Colonel Chipman commanding, from Savannah to Charleston. They will probably reach you to-day on the* [steamer] Coit. *The rest of this regiment is already with General Potter. If you can send Colonel Chipman's command out to General Hartwell with a reasonable prospect of its reaching him safely, you will do so. You will in such case instruct General Hartwell to communicate, if possible, with General Potter, and inquire whether General Potter desires Colonel Chipman's command to cross the Santee and join him. If General Potter replies affirmatively to this inquiry, General Hartwell will send Colonel Chipman's command forward to General Potter. If General Potter does not desire this addition to his force, Colonel Chipman will remain with General Hartwell. The major-general commanding thinks it desirable that General Potter's force be increased by this addition, and desires to impress upon you the necessity of a prompt and hearty cooperation by General Hartwell with General Potter, in case the latter is pressed and compelled to fall back toward the Santee.*[173]

Three days later, Hatch received the following communication from C.C. Nell aboard the naval transport *Augusta*, stationed off Wright's Bluff on the Santee River:

> [Potter] *is marching on this place, having had a fight at Sumterville, driving the enemy and capturing three pieces of artillery. The Federal forces on the south side of this river have seen nothing but a navy steam launch, which came up last night, reports them at a bluff about twenty miles from here below. As soon as I can get wood will send a steamer down there. The* Augusta, Savannah, General Hooker, *navy tug* Daffodil, *and three launches are here all out of coal. We have had no trouble on the river except the steam launch being fired on by musketry.*[174]

On April 25, Colonel Chipman reported back:

> *Taking the Monk's Corners road I arrived with my command at Nelson's Ferry at noon on the 13th instant, having met several detachments of the enemy's cavalry (after leaving Monk's Corners), which made slight resistance at first, but skirmishing sharply the forenoon of the 13th instant. On arriving at the ferry I learned from contrabands that General Hartwell had returned to Charleston two days before. I communicated with General Potter, then near Manchester, and received orders from him the 15th instant to join his command without delay at Statesburg or beyond. I found it impossible to cross at that place, when Lieutenant O'Kane, commanding gun-boat* Daffodil, *seeing my difficulty, took my command on board his boat to Wright's Bluff. We were fired upon by guerrilla parties from the bluffs during our passage up the river. Arrived at Wright's Bluff at 8.30 p.m., and marched the next morning (the 16th) for Statesburg; camped for the night at the Manning plantation. Arrived at Statesburg at noon the 17th, and hearing the enemy were in large force and fortifying at Swift Creek, and that General Potter had marched toward Bradford Springs, I marched in the same direction, following his trail, camping for the night near the Springs.*[175]

Unfortunately, Chipman did not know where Potter was, but since he "deemed it necessary to communicate with him," Chipman sent Lieutenant Charles L. Barrel with two orderlies, all mounted to find the raiders. After leaving camp, Lieutenant Barrell "met a Confederate colonel and his orderly; by his coolness and bravery succeeded in capturing the orderly, whom he made a guide to conduct him past the Confederate forces into our lines."[176]

On April 14, the raiders learned that the U.S. flag had been raised above Fort Sumter in Charleston Harbor, four years to the day after the war had begun. An inspection was made of the men that day where "instances of vandalism are reported of money & gold & silver being demanded of defenseless women."[177]

Pickets from the 54th Massachusetts found themselves under fire from a group of twenty Confederate skirmishers on the night of April 14, near Stateburg. Lieutenant Colonel Hooper took a large group from the regiment on a reconnaissance mission to scout the area, but after marching two miles toward Stateburg and not seeing any Confederates, they returned to camp.[178]

The next morning, the 54th made plans for an early march from the Singleton plantation but did not get started until 3:00 p.m., when the 32nd U.S. Colored Troops returned from Wright's Bluff. The 25th Ohio was ordered to Stateburg as an advance for the division. Upon arriving there, they encountered more Confederates and drove them to Round Hill. From there, the Confederates

Stateburg, Sumter County, South Carolina, where Potter's men were able to quickly chase away a small group of Confederates with a bayonet charge on April 15. *Photo by the author.*

dug in, and the Union troops were unable to dislodge them.[179]

Potter came up with his main force and sent the 107th Ohio to join the 25th Ohio and make a demonstration against the Confederates. Meanwhile, the rest of the forces took a road to the right of the Confederate defenders and flanked them. Once again, a bayonet charge from the 25th Ohio dislodged the Confederates. The division stopped marching around midnight that night at Jenning's Swamp and Providence Post Office (modern-day Dalzell), having marched twelve miles that day. Potter would later write that he drove "the enemy back far enough to uncover a road leading to the main road between Sumterville and Camden, and gained the latter road by a night march."[180]

Before leaving the Singleton plantation, Potter told Chipman to "at once take measures to join this command. You will proceed from Nelson's Ferry with your force up the Santee road, and join the column at Stateburg or beyond. All possible expedition will be used."[181]

On the sixteenth, the Second Brigade left Providence and marched toward Bradford Springs. Captain Emilio described the route as "a hilly and rolling country sparsely settled with poor whites." The weather was good. They arrived at the springs early in the afternoon and paused to have lunch there. After resting, they resumed their march and were harassed for the rest of the afternoon by Confederate skirmishers "who gave away readily, but kept a running fight all the afternoon." As a result, two members of the 54th

Massachusetts were killed, while one Confederate was killed and another captured. At the end of the day, the brigade was at Springs Hill, having marched sixteen miles.[182]

Spring Hill was the site of the Davis home. In the basement was an ill, elderly woman being looked after by her granddaughters. When the Confederates evacuated, the house was overrun by Federals. Luckily for the family, General Potter arrived on the scene and, after making sure that there were no Confederates hiding, had a guard placed on the house and his surgeon sent to tend to the woman. However, she refused all medicine and accepted only a little food "from the hand of the enemy."[183]

Major Culp was not too impressed with the area, writing, "The land was poor, and the inhabitants mainly 'white trash'—not as intelligent as the negroes." Potter made the Davis house his headquarters for the night, where his surgeon used a door from an outbuilding as an operating table to amputate a leg. When Potter's men left the next morning, they took many of the family's valuables.[184]

Watching Potter was Colonel Colcock and his 3rd South Carolina Cavalry. Colcock had positioned himself along the Lynches River,

St. Phillip's Episcopal Church, Dalzell, South Carolina. Potter's men camped on the grounds of this church, established in 1840, en route to Spring Hill. *Photo by the author.*

believing that the raiders would march toward Bishopville and then move into North Carolina to join Sherman's army. However, when he learned that Potter was headed to Camden instead, he fled to try to find the raiders. Due probably to a lack of horses, Colcock abandoned his single piece of artillery at the edge of a swamp, where it had been pointed toward a road.[185]

Spring Hill, Lee County, South Carolina. On April 16, Potter's men clashed with Confederate cavalrymen here. *Photo by the author.*

Also on April 16, Gilmore sent messages to Major General Henry Halleck, chief of staff of the U.S. Army in Washington, and General Sherman apprising them of the raid's progress. To Halleck, he wrote:

> *I have a dispatch from General Potter, commanding the expedition sent to the interior of South Carolina, dated Sumterville, April 10. He met there a brigade of the enemy on its way to join Johnston, and routed them, capturing 3 pieces of artillery and losing but 30 men. Potter's cavalry has gone to Manchester, whither he will follow, and then determine his future movements. He is moving in a part of the country not touched by General Sherman; has destroyed immense amounts of property, including bridges, railroad buildings, and rolling-stock, cotton, lumber, and Government supplies. I shall carry out all General Sherman's instructions in that quarter.*[186]

Writing to Sherman, Gilmore noted:

> *I have a dispatch from General Potter, commanding the expedition sent to the interior of South Carolina, dated Sumterville, April 10. He met there a brigade of the enemy on its way to join Johnston, and routed them, capturing 3 pieces of artillery and losing but 30 men. Potter's cavalry has gone to Manchester, whither he will follow, and then determine his future operations. He is moving in a part of the country not touched by any of our armies, and has destroyed immense amounts of property, including bridges, railroad buildings, and rolling-stock, cotton, lumber, and Government supplies. I think all your instructions will be carried out in that quarter.*[187]

Potter arrived in Camden on April 17 and entered the town from the south "without opposition," despite rumors of five thousand Confederates between him and Camden. The Second Brigade entered the town first, followed by the First Brigade. Potter's men were greeted by local authorities, who surrendered the town to him. The raiders marched through the streets with the colors flying and the 157th New York band playing "John Brown's Body."[188] There was not much for Potter there, as Sherman's men had raided

Camden, South Carolina. Potter occupied this town on April 17. The raid's farthest point was this town, which had been visited by Sherman's army the previous February. *Photo by the author.*

the town almost two months earlier. More importantly, none of the railroad equipment he was expecting to find was there. "The railroad trains had been moved down below Boykin's Mill on Swift Creek," wrote Potter. "It was ascertained that the rolling-stock had been sent below during our advance from Singleton's, making success assured, though fighting was expected," wrote Captain Emilio after the war.[189]

Although Potter's men "broke into the banks and safes and did desultory damages," they were "restrained from general pillage of residences."[190]

Chapter 4

The Battle of Boykin's Mill and the Last Shots Fired

On April 18, still hoping and trying to find the elusive railroad equipment, Potter had his men leave Camden and march to Stateburg. "They departed hurriedly" around 7:00 a.m., "owing to the menace in their rear from…home guards who had been joined by some five hundred Kentucky cavalry of generals [Joseph Horace] Lewis and [Moses Wright] Hannon, and who had occupied the roads and crossings over Swift Creek along their line of communications." Barlow described it as "another hot and dusty march."[191]

While Potter had been waiting for supplies, the Confederates had been busy gathering up every able-bodied person they could find. Two brigades of cavalry under Major General Pierce Manning Butler Young had arrived in the area with Hannon's Brigade from Major General Joseph Wheeler's cavalry, which contained the 53rd Alabama and 11th Georgia Cavalry and two guns from Hannon's artillery. One Federal estimate put his forces at four hundred men.[192]

Young was born in Spartanburg, South Carolina, in 1836 but grew up in Georgia. He attended the Georgia Military Institute and West Point but resigned from the latter just months before graduating when Georgia seceded from the Union. He joined the Confederate army and rose from a second lieutenant of artillery in 1861 to a commander of a cavalry division under Major General Wade Hampton III in 1864. He had been commended for his "remarkable gallantry" during the Maryland Campaign.[193]

Meanwhile, Potter's main body moved along the road from Camden, and the 107th Ohio marched on a nearby railroad bed. They marched for

Major General Pierce M.B. Young. Young, shown here in a postwar photo, was the most senior and experienced Confederate officer to challenge the raiders, but he had too few soldiers to affect a successful stand at Boykin's Mill. *Courtesy of the Library of Congress.*

seven miles with only slight resistance until they came to Swift Creek, where Boykin's Mill and millpond were located. "There the enemy held earthworks running through a swamp and over the higher ground beyond the creek. The Confederates were posted on the south side of the creek, along the pond and back of a church. A cannon was placed in the south side of the stream which commanded the railroad crossing, the creek, the swamp and the Federal position. Behind a miller's house, on rising ground, was another cannon aimed at a highway 700 yards below the millpond dam which was the Federals route."[194]

To slow the Union advance, the Confederates opened the dam floodgates, flooding both the road and the swamp. Some Federals attempted to close the gates but were easily picked off by the Confederate defenders. Then, cannon fire started raining down on the Federals.[195]

Potter, using his main force in front as a diversion, sent the 54th Massachusetts, the 102nd U.S. Colored Troops and the 107th Ohio to the right of the creek with a local guide, only to learn "that the swamp was impassable." There were two streams, the first of which had water seven feet

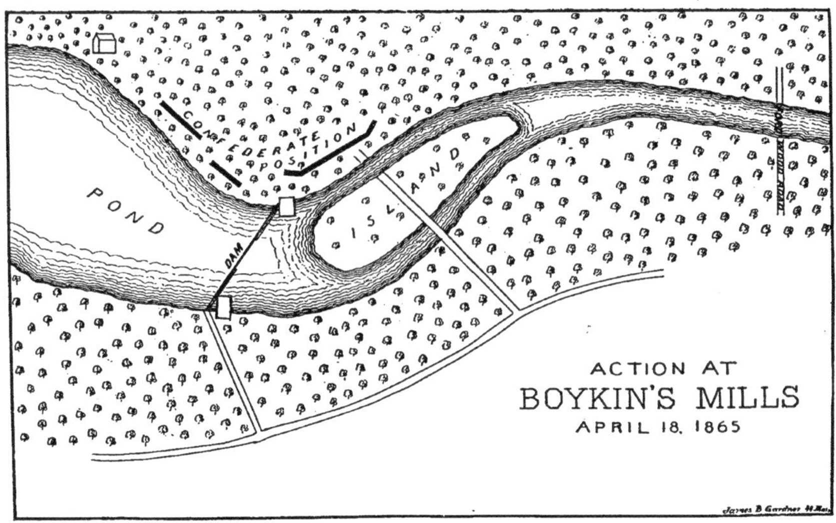

Map of the Battle of Boykin's Mill, Kershaw County, South Carolina. This map of the April 18, 1865 battle was originally published in *History of the Fifty-Fourth Regiment of Massachusetts Volunteer Infantry. Courtesy of the Walker Local History and Family History Center, Richland Library, Columbia, South Carolina.*

Site of the Battle of Boykin's Mill, Kershaw County, South Carolina. The battle took place to the left of the milldam shown in this picture. *Photo by the author.*

Swift Creek Baptist Church, Boykin's Mill, Kershaw County, South Carolina. Confederate cavalrymen were stationed behind this circa 1827 church. *Photo by the author.*

deep while the second stream had water that was waist deep. Eventually, the Federals located a favorable road, only to discover the Confederates waiting for them behind cotton bales.[196]

Riding a white horse, Lieutenant Edward L. Stevens of the 54th Massachusetts ordered his company to fire a volley at the Confederates. Colonel Artimus Darby Goodwyn observed this and asked his fifteen-year-old courier, Burwell H. Boykin, "Do you think you can stop him?" Young Boykin took carful aim and shot the lieutenant in the head, killing him instantly. His body fell into Swift Creek, forcing two men to risk their lives to recover it, and it now lies at the Florence National Cemetery. [197]

Lieutenant Stevens has the dubious distinction of being the last Federal officer killed in the war. He was honored by his alma mater, Harvard University, in its Memorial Hall. Years after the war, Stevens's fiancée asked Boykin to show her where her beau had been killed, unaware that the man she was asking was the person who had killed him. Boykin did, without admitting that he was the man who had done the deed.[198]

Shown at the bottom right in this photograph is Lieutenant Edward L. Stevens, 54th Massachusetts Infantry. The Harvard graduate is generally believed to be the last Union officer killed in the Civil War. Image taken from *History of the Fifty-Fourth Regiment of Massachusetts Volunteer Infantry. Courtesy of the Walker Local History and Family History Center, Richland Library, Columbia, South Carolina.*

While the Federals were flanking the Confederates, Lieutenant Colonel Hooper had the 54th Massachusetts try to capture the ground around the mill and a nearby bridge that covered the Confederates earthworks. He also had them capture a dam that was keeping the ground flooded, in case the flanking movement failed. However, it was decided that it would still be a risky crossing, so a cannon was requested and received by Hooper, who used it to clear away Confederate opposition in front of him.[199]

The Federals then charged the field. The desperate Confederates responded with cannon fire, using old iron chain and gravel for ammunition. But it was not enough, as the Federals eventually flanked the Confederates and forced them to retreat.[200] Captain Emilio wrote, "[The Confederates] contested the ground at Boykin's Mill…but after considerable firing, being outnumbered and out flanked, fell back to Dinkin's Mill." Potter simply wrote that he "found the enemy intrenched on the opposite side of a mill pond and swamp. After several attempts at different points a crossing was at length effected by the One hundred and second U.S. Colored Troops, and the rebels at once gave way."[201]

In a more detailed account dated April 26, Potter wrote:

> *No opposition was encountered until we reached Boykin's Mill on Swift Creek. The road here leads close by the mill, with mill-ponds and*

The grave of Lieutenant Stevens, Florence National Cemetery, Florence, South Carolina. This nondescript headstone marks the final resting place of the last Federal officer killed in the Civil War. Stevens's remains were originally buried on the battle site and were later moved to this location. *Photo by the author.*

swamps on the left and swamp on the right extending to the Wateree. The rebels had cut the dam, flooding the road, and had taken up the bridge across the stream. The land on the opposite side was higher and the enemy had thrown up an epaulement for two guns and an infantry parapet. The railroad crossed the swamp 300 yards to the right of the highway, and here also were rifle trenches. Hallowell's brigade was in advance, and the skirmishers of the Thirty-second U.S. Colored Troops were pushed forward into the swamp, but the water was too deep for them to effect a crossing. The One hundred and seventh Ohio, of Brown's brigade, was ordered to try to turn the enemy's right, but the creek could not be forded. The Fifty-fourth Massachusetts Volunteers was sent down to find a passage on the enemy's left. They discovered the remains of a bridge which had been burned, and in attempting to cross on a stringer, which was still standing, they received a sharp fire from the rebels posted behind intrenchments, and lost several men. The Twenty-fifth Ohio was placed on the edge of the swamp between the railroad and highway, ready to charge across the railroad. The detachment of the One hundred and second U.S. Colored Troops (Major Clark commanding) was ordered to get through on the left of the Fifty-fourth Massachusetts, and by the aid of a negro guide they succeeded in crossing on a log. The One hundred and seventh Ohio was at once ordered to their support. The other regiments were ordered to make a dash from their respective positions, which was done, and the enemy gave way.[202]

The 54th Massachusetts reported fifteen casualties: two men, Lieutenant Stevens and one enlisted man, were killed; another enlisted man was mortally wounded; and twelve others were injured. This was the largest loss suffered by any regiment during Potter's raid. Captain Emilio would write, "The charge was a plucky affair under adverse circumstances."[203]

After the fighting ended around 4:00 p.m., the Federals destroyed fifty-four bales of cotton and three bales of corn fodder. They also burned a gristmill and a sawmill. Unfortunately, though, Potter discovered that the trains had moved farther on down the road.[204]

Before the day was out, Potter skirmished again at Bradford's Springs. It rained that night, and the 157th New York found itself camping in "a half-flooded cornfield" three miles from the battlefield.[205]

Meanwhile, Colonel Chipman was fighting his way through the South Carolina interior, trying to join Potter. He later described his efforts:

Brisk skirmishing commenced with the enemy's cavalry on the morning of the 18th at different places, who made spirited resistance, fighting behind breast-works of rails, which they would not leave until driven from them by my skirmishers. We were hemmed in on every side, but moved steadily forward. My loss during the forenoon was 1 man killed, and 1 officer and

Site of the Battle of Dinkin's Mill, Sumter County, South Carolina. A short skirmish was fought here on April 19. *Photo by the author.*

> *7 men wounded. At 11 a.m. Lieutenant Barrell joined me, accompanied by Major Webster and detachment of his cavalry. They had driven the enemy from my front, and gave information concerning the movements of General Potter's forces. Skirmishing with my rear guard was kept up till afternoon. I joined the command of General Potter at 8 p.m. at Swift Creek, where my regiment was united.*[206]

Potter continued moving back toward Sumter, searching for the trains along the Camden Railroad, which connected Camden with Sumter. On April 19, he spent much of the day skirmishing with Young's Confederates. They first encountered them at Dinkin's Mill on Rafting Creek, where the Confederates were posted behind breastworks made of rails with one piece of artillery. According to Barlow, "the stream was too deep for fording," though Potter would claim that "the Twenty-fifth Ohio and One hundred and fifty-seventh New York charged through water waist-deep and drove [the Confederates] in complete rout."[207]

In his official report, Potter wrote:

After marching a short distance on the 19th the enemy's skirmishers were met behind barricades in the road, from which they were driven by our skirmishers. A little farther on we met with some slight resistance, the enemy opening from two guns in the road. He soon withdrew and fell back to the other side of Rafting Creek, at Dingle's Mill. The position resembled that at Boykin's Mill. The mill dam had been opened and the swamp was not fordable, while in the road the water was waist-deep, and any force attempting to cross here was exposed to a fire from the enemy behind rifle-trenches and with two guns commanding the road. Colonel Baird, with four companies of the Thirty-second U.S. Colored Troops, and the One hundred and seventh Ohio Volunteers, Lieutenant-Colonel Cooper, was moving down the railroad, which at this point is a mile distant from the high road, and was threatening to cross. Colonel Hallowell was directed to order Colonel Chipman, with the One hundred and second U.S. Colored Troops and four companies of the Thirty-second U.S. Colored Troops, to make a detour of several miles to our left, which would turn the swamp and bring him in the enemy's rear. About noon musketry was heard on the other side, followed by the fire of the enemy's guns. Brown's brigade was at once pushed over and the enemy retreated in great haste, one of his brigades, with the wagon train and artillery, taking the road toward Providence, while the other brigade kept the road to Statesburg.[208]

Later that day, as rains started to fall, Potter's men encountered the Confederates again at Beech Creek near Stateburg but quickly chased them away after some light fighting. This skirmish has the distinction of being the last shots of the Civil War fired in South Carolina, the state where the war began. By the time the Confederates reached Stateburg, they were "dispersed," probably because the Confederate leaders knew that any further attempt to resist Potter would be a futile waste of lives. At 10:00 p.m., the 54th Massachusetts returned to its former camp at the Singleton plantation.[209]

Potter wrote, "At Beech Creek, a short distance to the northward of Statesburg, [the Confederates] made another stand, but the Twenty-fifth Ohio and One hundred and fifty-seventh New York charged through water waist-deep and drove him in complete rout. We moved on to Middleton Depot, and there found the railroad trains we were seeking." A detachment from the 4th Massachusetts cavalry pursued the Confederates for four or five miles, capturing a number of prisoners in the process and breaking up the last Confederate resistance in South Carolina.[210]

Site of the Battle of Beech Creek, Sumter County, South Carolina. The last shots of the Civil War within the Palmetto State were fired here on April 19, 1865. *Photo by the author.*

Today, much of the site of the Battle of Beech Creek is a golf course. *Photo by the author.*

Oakland Plantation, Sumter County, South Carolina. This historic plantation home was used by both Young and Potter as their headquarters on April 18 and 19, respectively. *Photo by the author.*

Potter himself spent the night of April 19 at Oakland Plantation, which had been the headquarters for General Young just twenty-four hours earlier. Besides being Potter's headquarters, the house was also used as a field hospital.[211]

On the twentieth, the 25th Ohio and the 157th New York "found the object of all the marching and counter-marching" at Middleton Depot, where the railroad engines and cars that had been abandoned by their engineers and crews at the broken-up railroad prevented the equipment from being moved any farther. According to Culp, "for two miles the [rail]road was crowded with cars, including sixteen locomotives. The cars were loaded with clothing, ammunition, provisions, and, in fact, everything imaginable." Culp placed the numbers at seventeen locomotives and one hundred cars. According to Potter, "18 locomotives were destroyed and 200 cars, more than half of them being filled with subsistence, ordnance, and quartermaster's stores and railway machinery." In addition, rations and naval stores were found, and some much-needed shoes were taken from the supplies. The Federals loaded some cars with gunpowder and others with shells and then set them afire.

"The explosion was terrific," wrote Culp, "and for several hours it seemed as if a battle was being fought." Barlow wrote, "There was a lovely popping when the shells began to explode." After finishing its work, the regiment returned to Singleton.[212]

After the war, Captain Emilio reflected:

> *Fighting was now over. The rolling-stock was ours, massed on the Camden Branch, whence it could not be taken, as the Fifty-fourth had destroyed the trestle at Wateree Junction, on the 11th. General Potter devoted the 20th to its destruction. That day the Fifty-fourth marched to Middleton Depot and with other regiments assisted in the work. About this place for a distance of some two miles were sixteen locomotives and 245 cars containing railway supplies, ordnance, commissary and quartermaster's stores. They were burned, those holding powder and shells during several hours blowing up with deafening explosions and scattering discharges, until property of immense value and quantity disappeared in smoke and flame. Locomotives were rendered useless before the torch was applied. The Fifty-fourth alone destroyed fifteen locomotives, one passenger, two box and two platform cars with the railway supplies they held. After completing this work, the regiment returned to Singleton's. Every purpose of the movement* [had] *been accomplished.*[213]

Sherman telegrammed Gilmore on the nineteenth "that he has concluded a convention with General Johnston subject to approval of the terms at Washington, whereby the Confederate armies are to be disbanded, and in his judgment lasting peace will be secured. He directs that our forces in this department cease all further destruction of public and private property. While you are to execute this order literally, still the major-general commanding directs that you suppress every manifestation of rebellious or disloyal feeling within your command."[214]

Meanwhile, back in Hilton Head, Gilmore ordered Brigadier General John Porter Hatch to send the 102nd U.S. Colored Troops who were not with Potter to hold the railroad bridge over the Santee River. Potter would be ordered to send the rest to rendezvous there to reunite the entire regiment with Colonel Chipman. The reunited regiment would be under Hatch's command.[215] More significantly, "General Potter is ordered to cease all further destruction of public and private property within the rebel lines, and to return to Georgetown, or march down to Charleston, as may be in his judgment most feasible. The orders to General Potter are sent to you with this. You will forward them to him as soon as possible by flag of truce."[216]

Meanwhile, many families throughout Sumter County had sought refuge at Millford, the home of former South Carolina governor John Laurence Manning, located near Pinewood, South Carolina. On the morning of April 21, people there saw the smoke of seven hundred bales of cotton burning at a nearby plantation. Soon a noisy band of black troops came into the house and asked Manning if he had any protection for the house.[217] "Our only protection is from the army of the Confederate States," the former governor responded, to which one of the soldiers raised his gun at the elderly man and said, "You are a dead man." But before a shot could be fired, there was a shout: "Halt! The general is at the front door."[218]

The governor walked outside his front door and greeted Potter, who informed him that he "had come to protect your family and home from injury." To this, Manning replied, "I ask no protection but for the ladies under my roof and that is always granted in civilized warfare." To which Potter responded, "That is my object in coming here and I'll carry out my purpose."[219]

The general entered the house and complimented Manning on it. The former governor told the general, "It was built by a man from England by

Milford, Pinewood, South Carolina, circa 1900. Built between 1839 and 1841, this national landmark is considered one of the finest examples of Greek Revival architecture in the United States. Potter visited here on April 21 on his way back to Georgetown. *Courtesy of the Walker Local History and Family History Center, Richland Library, Columbia, South Carolina.*

the name of Potter, and I suppose a man from New York by the name of Potter will destroy it." However, the general said, "No sir, that is not my intention. Your place shall be protected."[220]

Potter issued orders that everything on the premise should be protected and, in a tone that all could hear, said, "There shall be no injury done to your estate, Governor, and the ladies shall be protected." He also threatened to hang two soldiers who tried to steal a horse.[221]

Potter asked Manning if he had heard any news about the fall of the Confederacy, to which the governor replied no. Potter then went inside, where he and his staff were presented to the ladies of the house.[222]

Potter and his staff visited with the Mannings for six hours, leaving around 4:00 p.m. after Potter's raiders had passed by and making sure there were no stragglers. During their stay, the Federal officers were given a tour of the home and engaged in lively conversation.[223]

On April 20, Young was told of the armistice and was ordered to inform Potter of this under a flag of truce. There are conflicting accounts regarding Potter's receiving news of Johnston's surrender to Sherman. Captain Emilio claimed:

> *While we were at* [Manning's] *plantation, a Confederate officer came to the outposts with a flag of truce, to notify General Potter that an armistice had been concluded between Generals Sherman and Johnston. Hostilities were not to be renewed without forty-eight hours' notice. This great news created the most intense joy and excitement, for it seemed to end the war, as the Rebels themselves acknowledged. Cheers without number were given, and congratulations exchanged. Then the Fifty-fourth was brought to a field, where the last shots loaded with hostile intent were fired as a salute.*[224]

However, Major Culp claimed that before reaching the plantation house, the Federals had skirmished with a small group of Confederates. After chasing them away, the raiders were resting by a swamp when "a rebel officer, Col. Rhett, came to our rear guard under a white flag, and desired to see General Potter, saying he was bearing dispatches from General [P.G.T.] Beauregard, announcing that Generals Lee and Johnson had surrendered, and that the war was over."[225]

However, another account claims that twenty minutes after Potter left, a Confederate courier named Lieutenant Rhett rode up to the house and told them of Confederate general Joseph Johnston's surrender to General William T. Sherman outside Durham, North Carolina.[226] According to this version, the courier, exhausted from his ride, fell asleep almost immediately on a divan in the hallway but was awakened by the governor and asked to go to Potter under a flag of truce. The lieutenant complied and found Potter only a mile away. Potter returned the courier to Manning with one of his own aides to convey his compliments and good wishes to the governor. By the time the two men returned to the Manning plantation, there were about sixty Confederates who had heard the news wanting to learn more.[227]

Potter himself said that on April 21, "we began moving toward Georgetown by the Santee road, and at noon of that day I received a dispatch by flag of truce from Major-General Young, stating that a truce had been agreed upon on the 19th instant between Generals Johnston and Sherman." In a subsequent report, Potter wrote:

> *On the 21st the march was taken up for Georgetown by the way of the Santee River road. At 1 p.m., while the column was halted at Fulton Post-Office, I received a communication by flag of truce from Major-General Young, commanding the force which had been opposed to us, stating that a truce had been agreed upon between Generals Johnston and Sherman, and that notice of forty-eight hours would be given prior to the resumption of hostilities. I answered that my command was moving toward Georgetown, and that it would no longer subsist on the country, except in the matter of forage for animals.*[228]

Corporal Barlow's account substantiates Potter, as he claimed that they were at Fulton's Post Office, which was only a short distance from Milford, when around noon a Confederate courier with a flag of truce came up to the raiders and told them the news. "Cheer on cheer went up from the troops. The news seemed too good to be true. All foraging was prohibited; the guns were discharged and with a white flag at the head of the column the return march was begun, and at night the men halted near a large mill, having made eighteen miles."[229]

That same day, Gilmore dispatched the following message to Potter:

> *I have the honor to inform you that on the 19th instant Major-General Sherman, who was then at Raleigh, N.C., instructed me that he had concluded a convention with General Johnston, subject to an approval of the terms at Washington, whereby the Confederate armies are to be disbanded, and in his (General Sherman's) judgment a lasting peace will be secured. Until such approval is obtained or further orders received a cessation of hostilities within*

> *this department is ordered. You are accordingly instructed on the receipt of this to cease from all further destruction of public and private property. You will forthwith return to Georgetown or march down to Charleston, as may in your judgment be most feasible. You will, after receiving this order, conduct your march as if in a friendly country, observing, of course, suitable precautions against surprise or treachery. You will direct that part of the One hundred and second U.S. Colored Troops which is with you to join Colonel Chipman and the balance of the regiment at the railroad bridge across the Santee River. General Hatch has been ordered to send Colonel Chipman and such part of his regiment as is with him to form a post at the bridge. This post will constitute a part of the command of General Hatch.*[230]

On the twenty-second, as the troops marched down the Santee Road, they came opposite of Wright's Bluff. There, "the wounded, sick, and about five hundred contrabands were sent to the river for transportation by water."[231] Also that day, Potter received official word of Lee's surrender, which "though not unexpected, caused great rejoicing," according to Captain Emilio. Major Culp wrote, "The joy that filled our hearts was supreme." Potter turned over command of the division to Lieutenant Colonel Brown and departed for Hilton Head. Colonel Carmichael replaced Brown as brigade commander. After a twenty-three-mile march, the troops halted for the night.[232]

The division moved out at 5:30 a.m. the next morning. Because the war was apparently over, the troops were forbidden to fire unless under attack. They could also no longer seize supplies and instead had to purchase them. Making the supply problems even worse was the number of escaped slaves following the raiders, hampering their march. Despite this, however, they were able to make another twenty-three-mile march.[233]

Also on the twenty-third, Potter's men received word of Lincoln's death. "Sad tidings which could hardly be credited," wrote Emilio. "There was much bitter feeling indulged in by the soldiery for a time."[234]

However, the sad tidings had to be set aside for solving the supply issue. On April 24, the raiders marched through "a wooden region where no supplies could be obtained. As a substitute for rations two ears of corn were issued to each man." Despite their growling stomachs, the men still made twenty-three miles that day. They reached Leunds Ferry, only to discover that the boats with rations and supplies that were supposed to be waiting for them there had gone back to Charleston.[235]

Barlow was not too happy about his rations or the man who issued the orders for them: "Certainly almost any other man in the colonel's position would have found means and fed his faithful soldiers on other than horse feed, in such a land of plenty. Col. Brown was an excellent man, only, he failed in acute discernment, sometimes." The two ears of corn were served for supper and breakfast.[236]

The raiders broke camp for the last time on April 25. At noon, they were met with wagons from Georgetown. After marching twenty-two miles, Potter's men reached Georgetown sometime between 5:00 and 6:00 p.m. The raid was over.[237]

On April 26, from Hilton Head, Potter reported:

> *Our loss will not exceed eighty. The enemy's loss is very much larger. The troops fought and marched remarkably well. The results of the expedition may be summed up as follows: Captured, 3 guns, 1 battle-flag, 50 prisoners, and 300 horses and mules; destroyed, 32 locomotives, 250 cars, large quantities of Government stores, all the railway stations, freight houses, and machine-shops between Camden and Maysville, large portions of the railway between those points, and 2,500 bales of cotton. The number of negroes who followed the column may be estimated at 5,000.*[238]

On May 6, Potter wrote:

> *The results of the expedition may be summed up in the capture of 1 battle-flag, 3 guns, and 65 prisoners, 100 horses and 150 mules, and the destruction of 32 locomotives, 250 cars, large portions of the railroad, and all the railroad buildings between Camden and Sumterville, 100 cotton gins and presses, 5,000 bales of cotton, and large quantities of government stores. Five thousand negroes joined the column and were brought within our lines. Our entire loss was 10 killed, 72 wounded, and 1 missing.*
>
> *In conclusion I cannot too highly praise the conduct of officers and men during this expedition. They bore with cheerfulness the fatigue of a long and toilsome march, made more arduous by the constant skirmishing, and in our frequent encounters with the enemy displayed great dash and courage.*
>
> *The brigade commanders, Colonel Brown and Colonel Hallowell, were at all times prompt and efficient in the discharge of their duties.*[239]

Gilmore endorsed Potter's April 26 report, writing, "General Potter's conduct of the expedition to Sumterville has been characterized by great energy, skill, and foresight, and has been eminently successful."[240]

In all, the raiders had marched about three hundred miles in twenty-one days. "The estimate placed on property destroyed by that raid, including cotton, cotton-gins, presses and buildings, was at least one million dollars."[241]

They also returned to Georgetown with thousands of former slaves while freeing an additional three thousand. The slaves were described as "poor people who had been slaves and all their worldly goods were few. Some carried everything they owned balanced in bundles on their heads. Others had horses or mules laden, and some had carts in which the chickens and the little freedmen shared the privilege of transportation." The newly freed slaves were given a few days' rations and then advised to go back home, as the war was over and they would now be paid for their labors.[242]

Corporal Barlow waxed poetically about his company:

> *Co. G returned to duty, as of old and the time passed pleasantly. Hard marching made them feel a bit old and some of them believed that an inch or two was taken from the stature of each man, but the suspicion was not confirmed. A few had lost flesh and the tobacco chewers, who had reveled in the weed, might have gained a few pounds. Some had grown handsomer from roasting in the sun; certainly none had grown homelier. Co. G had no homely men. The only man who could have been called really homely, had deserted. Probably he was lonely.*[243]

On April 26, Gilmore told Sherman, "General Potter's expedition to Sumterville and Camden has been very successful. He destroyed 32 locomotives and 250 cars. The destruction was most complete." He ended the note with some unintended irony: "[Potter] did not find it necessary to go to Florence, as the rolling-stock of the railroad was all between Sumterville, Manchester, and Camden, with but a trifling exception."[244]

Chapter 5

The Raid Ends and the War Winds Down

While waiting to hear back from Sherman, Gilmore made plans to send Potter's command to Charleston, save for a small garrison to hold Georgetown. "Send the cavalry dismounted to Hilton Head and mount infantry in their stead. All captured animals will be sent to Hilton Head except what are required to mount the infantry. The command will be prepared for another raid. The quartermaster's department will furnish transportation," wrote Gilmore.[245]

That raid was probably intended for Augusta, Georgia. On April 17, Gilmore had told Sherman:

> *As soon as the expedition from Sumterville returns I would like to strike for Augusta, Ga. I believe I could get together a sufficient force for that purpose without more troops, but to make the thing certain and complete I should have 2,000 or 3,000 more men and some cavalry. The small squad of cavalry which I have is all ordered to City Point. It occurs to me that you may now be in condition to spare the 4,000 troops sent to North Carolina from my command, or a portion of them. If you cannot give me any more men I am disposed to try it with what I have, and await your instructions and authority to go in person, if I deem it best.*[246]

But by April 21, Gilmore was thinking about another destination, telling Hatch that he wanted "to occupy Branchville as soon as General Potter's force is available. You will receive further orders as to this." Branchville, located near Orangeburg, was where the South Carolina Railroad, the rail line that connected Augusta with Charleston, had a spur that led to Columbia. Federal officials had been so desirous of taking it that Sherman was told to aim for it, should he be unable to capture Savannah. However, Sherman chose to bypass Branchville for Midway, concerned that Branchville might be too heavily fortified.[247]

Despite the apparent cessation of hostilities, Gilmore told Sherman on April 27, "General Potter's command has returned to Georgetown, and I wish to keep it moving, but do not know whether you want me to strike for any particular place or not. I can move it to any place within the States of South Carolina or Georgia. If Wilson's cavalry is not to go to Augusta perhaps I had better send it there. I will wait three or four days to hear from you."

However, three days later, Potter was ordered by Sherman

> *to proceed to Orangeburg, S.C., with the forces hitherto under your command, excepting the garrison left at Georgetown. The One hundred and second U.S. Colored Troops, heretofore ordered to the Santee railroad bridge, will accompany you. You will move as soon as you have collected 1,000 men of your command; the balance will follow as rapidly as possible. You will rebuild the bridge over the Edisto at Orangeburg, making requisition for all necessary material. You will guard your communications with Charleston as far back as Summerville. General Hatch will protect the road to that point.*[248]

However, for reasons unknown, Potter never made it to Orangeburg. On May 6, Potter was in Beaufort, South Carolina, and five days later, he was in Hilton Head trying to help newly freed slaves and their former masters understand the new reality of a slave-free South Carolina. That day, Potter received word from Gilmore that he was to demand and receive

> *the surrender of all Confederate forces on your front, with all arms and public property in their possession or in any manner under their control. For making out the rolls of paroled prisoners and furnishing them with certificates of parole you will use the forms furnished herewith. You will forward your copy of these rolls to these headquarters and will also furnish inventories of all arms and public property received by you under the above-mentioned military convention.*[249]

This is the last assignment Potter received from the army during the war recorded in the *Official Records of the War of the Rebellion.*

By the first week of May, many of the raiders had been sent from Georgetown to Charleston. Hallowell was assigned command to what was wryly called the "Defences of Charleston," which was composed of the entrenched line around the city, St. Andrew's Parish and the James Island lines. Later, Mount Pleasant was included in his command. The troops under him were the 54th, 107th Ohio and 21st U.S. Colored Troops.[250]

Gilmore was very pleased with the raid, telling the War Department on May 23, "The expedition was, as heretofore reported by me, a complete success, and the manner of its execution reflects great credit upon General Potter, who conducted his delicate operations with equal bravery, discretion, and energy."[251] He recommended Potter for a brevet promotion to major general of the U.S. Volunteers to date from April 9, 1865, the day Potter captured Sumter. "[Potter's] former services during the war have been valuable, and his conduct during General Foster's operations upon the Charleston and Savannah Railroad, in November and December last, merited and received the highest commendation from General Hatch, his immediate, and General Foster, the department commander."[252]

Gilmore also recommended that Lieutenant Colonels Carmichael and Nathaniel Haughton of the 25th Ohio be promoted to full colonels by brevet, based on Potter's recommendations. He wrote:

> *Lieutenant-Colonel Carmichael's command captured a battle-flag and two guns in the fight at Dingle's Mill, on April 9, 1865. Lieutenant-Colonel Haughton distinguished himself in the fight at Boykin's Mill, near Camden, on April 18. Both officers, with their regiments, are also specially mentioned for their conduct in the battle near Statesburg* [on] *April 19. These officers distinguished themselves during last fall's operations in this department, and are truly brave and efficient soldiers.*[253]

Famed Civil War diarist Mary Chesnut returned to her Camden plantation home, Mulberry, in early May 1865. Upon her arrival, she lamented:

> *Sherman only took our horses. Potter's raid, which was after Johnston's surrender, ruined us final, burning our mills and gins and a hundred bales of cotton. Indeed nothing is left now but the bare land and debts made for the support of these hundreds of negroes during the war.*[254]

One Sumter resident, identified only as B. Hood, wrote on August 24, 1865, "We are under military rule and that of the worst kind and God only knows how long it will last. This has been a terrible war…you cannot imagine the devastation of property and suffering it has caused us."[255]

Per Gilmore's recommendation, Edward Potter was brevetted to major general, dating from March 15, 1865. He resigned his commission on July 24, 1865, and spent the rest of his life practicing law, alternating between New York City and Madison, New Jersey. Having never married, he died alone from pneumonia in a New York City boardinghouse on June 1, 1889. The funeral was held at New York's Grace Church, and he was buried in Manhattan's Marble Cemetery. A delegation from New York's Union Club, of which the general was a member, attended the services.[256]

Little is known about Colonel Philip P. Brown Jr.'s postwar life. He went on leave "up north" in June 1865. After leaving the army, he moved to St. Louis, where he was involved in "extensive businesses." The 1890 U.S. census lists him with a wife and daughter and working as a "confectioner." He died on April 8, 1881, from typhoid pneumonia at the age of fifty-eight.[257]

Colonel Edward Needles Hallowell was brevetted to rank of brigadier general for his service during the war on March 12, 1866, to date from June 27, 1865. He returned to his home state and became a merchant in the town of Medford, where he died on July 26, 1871, due in part from the wounds he received during the war.[258]

Major General Quincy Adams Gilmore resigned his volunteer commissions and became a major in the U.S. Army Corps of Engineers. He moved to New York City and became recognized in both military and civilian circles as one of the finest engineers in the county, authoring several well-received books and articles related to the subject. He also oversaw the repair and rebuilding of several coastal fortifications, including many he had helped to damage or destroy, and was involved in planning improvements for both harbors and trains. He was promoted to lieutenant colonel in 1874 and full colonel in 1883.

In his private life, Gilmore was a prominent member of the University Club of New York. Allegedly, he married the widow of Confederate general Braxton Bragg sometime after Bragg's death in 1876. He died on April 7, 1888, from liver and kidney problems that started during the siege of Charleston during the Civil War. His son and grandson, both named Quincy Gilmore, were also U.S. Army generals.[259]

Colonel Charles Colcock retreated into North Carolina, where he joined General Joseph Johnston's forces just in time for their surrender to Sherman.

After the war, he briefly lived in Savannah, where he tried to sell insurance. Afterward, he moved to Hampton County, South Carolina, where he enjoyed success growing cotton. He died in 1891.[260]

Major General Pierce Manning Butler Young returned to Georgia after the war. He served five terms in Congress, from 1868 until 1875, and held diplomatic posts in Russia, Guatemala and Honduras. He died in New York City on July 6, 1896, and was buried in Cartersville, Georgia, near his plantation.[261]

Two of Potter's raiders would go on to receive the Medal of Honor, the nation's highest military honor. Lieutenant Charles L. Barrell would be so honored on May 14, 1891, for "hazardous service in marching through enemy's country to bring relief to his command" in his attempt to established communications between Chipman and Potter.[262] On March 30, 1898, Private Henry S. Finkenbiner was awarded the Congressional Medal of Honor for his heroism at Dingle's Mill. His citation read, "While on the advance skirmish line and within direct and close fire of the enemy's artillery, [he] crossed the mill race on a burning bridge and ascertained the enemy's position."[263]

Though the Confederate States of America never gave out any medals during its short existence, the Sons of Confederate Veterans since 1977 have chosen to posthumously honor Confederate soldiers whose deeds have been deemed worthy of such recognition. Two of these have been awarded to Confederates who faced Potter's men.[264] In 1997, Lieutenant Raphael Painpare was honored for his heroism at the Battle of Dingle's Mill. In 1999, Lieutenant Charles H. Jones was honored for his heroics in Manning.[265]

Chapter 6

The Raid's Legacy

When examining Potter's raid, one must ask two questions:

(1) Was the raid necessary?
(2) Why has it been all but forgotten?

For the first question, with a century and a half of hindsight, the answer is clearly no. There was little of value left in the Palmetto State that could have aided the Confederate cause at this late stage in the war. Furthermore, given the damage to railroads in the Carolinas and Virginia, and the presence of two large Union armies between Richmond and South Carolina, it is very doubtful that the trains could have even made it to a place where they could have been of any use. Plus, just days into the campaign, Lee surrendered to Grant, effectively ending the war.

In fact, one of the raiders, Corporal Barlow, questioned the usefulness of the raid:

> *Enough comment has been made upon the merits of raids, burnings and destruction generally. But this raid in particular was practically uncalled for. On the very day the locomotives and cars were destroyed, Beauregard issued his order announcing the truce. The surrender of Johnston practically ended the war. And thus thousands and tens of thousands worth of property were destroyed needlessly.*[266]

However, he acknowledged, "But it was war, and so far justifiable."[267]

But even without the benefit of hindsight, Sherman's decision to order the raid still must be questioned. As mentioned, there were fewer than 1,500 able-bodied men in all of South Carolina, just barely enough to make a brigade and certainly not enough to turn the war toward the South's favor, a fact that Sherman almost certainly knew.

There are two possibilities, then. The first is that Sherman was worried about Johnston's forces, though he didn't need to be. Sherman would admit that he overestimated Johnston's forces in North Carolina at thirty-seven thousand, which was, at best, half the size of Sherman's force.[268] The far more likely argument is that Sherman was still smarting from the failed Florence raid and that his pride and/or ego refused to allow him to let the matter slide, which is very consistent with Sherman's often eccentric personality. (It can be argued that he was so fond of his men that he was overprotective of them.) The fact that Sherman was willing to sacrifice hard-won Southern ports being used by both the U.S. Army and Navy to see this mission done suggests that he might not have thought his idea through. Also, the fact that Sherman made no mention of the raid in his 1875 memoirs suggests that, upon further review, he did not consider it to be a significant action at all.[269]

As for the second question, at first glance, the reason why it is not as well known as other campaigns of the war is fairly obvious. First, the combined population of the five counties the raiders marched through was only 86,834 in 1860.[270] Second, the number of military personnel active in the raid and its battles was small, only 3,000 to 4,000 combined Union and Confederate troops. It is also worth noting that unlike many successful Union veterans of the war, neither Potter nor any of his brigade commanders ever sought political office, so there was no need for any of them to boast, talk or write about his military experiences. In fact, all of them spent their postwar years in relative obscurity. Third, the raid happened as the war was literally ending and had no effect on its outcome. Fourth, it came about a month after Sherman had completed his march through South Carolina, which left an indelible scar that has yet to fully heal. Fifth, there were no large battles during the raid, and none of the military leaders involved became household names.[271]

Also, there are very few surviving written accounts, correspondence and reports written at the time by the Confederate military leaders involved. This really is not surprising, given that the Confederate government was in exile and the two main Southern armies in the field had either surrendered or were negotiating surrender. In South Carolina, the situation was equally bad, as the governor had fled the state capital, and the military chain of command was virtually nonexistent. Consequently, there was hardly anyone or any place a Confederate officer could have sent a report to, and even if there had been, things happened so fast that there would not have been time to write one.

Furthermore, there were no journalists, illustrators or photographers accompanying the raid to leave a record of what went on. This is understandable, given the haste that went into organizing the raid. But even if journalists had been, as we say in the twenty-first century, "embedded" with Potter, their stories would have been pushed aside by the news of Lincoln's death and Lee's and Johnston's surrenders.

This means that most of the firsthand accounts written during or soon after the raid are from Union reports and dispatches filed in the *Official Records* or from postwar Northern regimental histories, the type of accounts that would have been looked on with suspicion in the postwar South for decades to come.

But as was mentioned in the introduction, even veterans of the conflict tended to forget or not talk about the event, as witnessed by the lack of coverage of the raid in publications that specialized in printing reminiscences of the war, such as the previously named *Confederate Veteran* and *Century Magazine*. Many of these publications are among the most popular and important sources for firsthand accounts of the Civil War, and the exclusion of Potter's Raid from them help doomed the event to the national obscurity it now has.

Also, one must ask if part of the reason why the raid was "forgotten" was because of the presence of African American troops. For white slave owners, the fact that they were now at the mercy of troops whose race they had held in bondage and felt superior to had to be a hard blow to their psyche. This might explain why they put the raid out of sight and out of mind. While there is no hard proof of this, there are some telling clues in the civilian accounts of the raid. In many of them, General Potter is described as a gentleman who kept order wherever he was. The white soldiers are often described as polite and sometimes even friendly. But the African American troops are almost always described with language that, even by the standards of the day, can be viewed only as hateful and racist. And while some of those in the raiders' path might have thought that the use of black troops was an intended insult to the white slaveholding elite,

Battle of Dingle's Mill monuments. The tall monument in the middle was first erected in 1913 and moved to this location in 1942. The cannons flanking the monument were erected in 1979 when the park was dedicated. *Photo by the author.*

it should be remembered that Potter's forces were hastily assembled from whatever units could be spared in Charleston, and there was probably little, if any, thought of any racial message or intent in selecting them. The case in point is presented by the false claims made by William Willis Boddie in his 1923 history of Williamsburg County: "Potter's raiders were composed of some organized Union forces, many self-attached robber bands, and hundreds of plantation deserting negro slaves."[272]

It was not until 1913, forty-eight years after the raid, that the first monument to it was erected at the site of the Battle of Dingle's Mill. It was moved in 1942 when the nineteenth-century road gave way to a modern highway. Today, it sits at the Battle of Dingle's Mill Memorial Park, surrounded by two cannons that were added when the park was dedicated in 1979.[273]

This was the only monument or marker to Potter's Raid until 1956, when the State of South Carolina placed a highway marker commemorating the Battle of Dingle's Mill. The next year, a state highway marker was erected

Battle of Boykin's Mill monument, Kershaw County, South Carolina. The obelisk, erected in 1995, lists the names of all the units involved in the battle and honors Lieutenant Stevens. The mill building in the background is a postwar structure. *Photo by the author.*

commemorating the Battle of Boykin's Mill. Six years later, in 1963, a marker was erected commemorating the skirmish at Spring Hill.[274]

No new markers commemorating the raid were erected for three decades, until 1993, when a marker was erected in Sumter to mark the spot of Potter's headquarters. Four years later, the site of the Battle of Beech Creek received a marker.[275]

In 1995, the 54th Massachusetts Reenactment Unit erected an Egyptian-style obelisk monument to the Battle of Boykin's Mill. The monument lists the names of all the units involved in the battle. It also honors Lieutenant Stevens and Private Boykin.[276]

In 1998, Alan D. Thigpin of Sumter published the 648-page *The Illustrated Recollections of Potter's Raid, April 5–21, 1865*, the first book ever dedicated to the subject. However, Thigpin's decision to simply "cut and paste" firsthand accounts of the raid along with some modern and contemporary photos and illustrations without adding any context, commentary or insight drew sharp criticism from the historical community. Furthermore, many critics

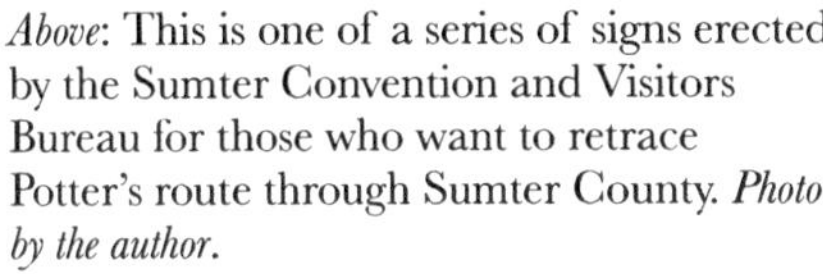

Above: This is one of a series of signs erected by the Sumter Convention and Visitors Bureau for those who want to retrace Potter's route through Sumter County. *Photo by the author.*

Right: A brochure on Potter's Raid written by local historian Robert Brown and produced by the Sumter County Historical Commission and the Sumter Convention and Visitors Bureau. *Author's collection.*

felt that much of the material was superfluous with little direct connection to the raid itself.[277]

In the twenty-first century, the Sumter County Historical Commission has been actively trying to promote awareness of the event. Toward this end, it erected historic markers in 2002 and 2006 throughout the county commemorating more places related to the raid. In addition, in 2005, with the help of the Sumter Convention and Visitors Bureau, the commission produced a brochure, written by local historian Robert Brown, that featured a driving tour of the raid throughout the county and nearby areas. The commission also erected signposts along the way where interested travelers could pick up the brochures.[278]

Two weeks after General Robert E. Lee surrendered to Lieutenant General Ulysses S. Grant at Appomattox Court House, Virginia, a letter writer to the Camden, South Carolina *Journal and Confederate* might have best summed up why Potter's Raid has been forgotten: "As always in the case in campaigning, there are many incidents we would like to record and preserve, but we have neither space nor time."[279]

Appendix
Military Units Involved in the Raid

Federal

Provisional Division
Brigadier General Edward Potter, commanding

First Brigade
Colonel Phillip P. Brown Jr., commanding

56th New York Infantry
157th New York Infantry
25th Ohio Infantry
107th Ohio Infantry

Second Brigade
Colonel Edward Needles Hallowell, commanding

Second Battalion, 4th Massachusetts Cavalry
54th Massachusetts Infantry
1st New York Engineers
Battery B, 3rd New York Artillery

32nd U.S. Colored Infantry
102nd U.S. Colored Infantry

CONFEDERATE*

Hannon's Brigade from Major General Joseph Wheeler's cavalry, which contained the 53rd Alabama and 11th Georgia Cavalry and two guns from Hannon's artillery

Two brigades of cavalry under Major General Pierce Manning Butler Young

1st Kentucky Brigade
9th Kentucky Mounted Regiment
3rd South Carolina Cavalry
20th South Carolina Militia
23rd South Carolina Infantry Regiment
mixed militia units and hospital convalescents

* Confederate forces opposing Potter were generally not well organized and were often hastily assembled, meaning that they had no official designation. Because of this and the scarceness of records, a completely accurate listing might not be possible.

Chronology

February 24, 1865—Georgetown, South Carolina, is captured by the U.S. Navy.

March 3—Major General William T. Sherman orders a cavalry raid on Florence, South Carolina, to destroy the railroad and rolling stock there.

March 4—A detachment of cavalry led by Colonel Reuben Williams leaves Cheraw, South Carolina, for Florence.

March 5—Williams's men are repulsed by a larger-than-expected Confederate force at Florence and are forced to flee back to Union lines.

March 6—Williams returns to Cheraw with his mission deemed a failure.

March 15—From Fayetteville, North Carolina, Sherman orders Major General Quincy Gilmore in Charleston, South Carolina, to launch another raid against South Carolina's inland railroads.

March 29—After being delayed due to poor weather, Gilmore starts making plans for the expedition.

April 1—Brigadier General Edward Potter arrives in Georgetown to take command of a provisional division that will participate in the raid.

April 2—General Robert E. Lee evacuates Richmond, Virginia, while Gilmore reviews the division.

April 4—Gilmore gives Potter his final instructions. South Carolina's Governor Andrew Gordon Magrath calls out the state militia to meet the threat posed by Potter's men.

April 5—The expedition leaves Georgetown.

April 8—Potter's men occupy Manning, South Carolina.

April 9—Battle of Dingle's Mill, outside Sumter, South Carolina. Lee surrenders to Lieutenant General Ulysses S. Grant at Appomattox Court House, Virginia.

April 9–10—Potter's men occupy Sumter.

April 11–15—Manchester, South Carolina, occupied by Potter's men.

April 14—President Abraham Lincoln is shot while attending a play in Washington, D.C. He dies the next morning.

April 16—Skirmish at Spring Hill.

April 17—Camden, South Carolina, occupied; Confederate general Joseph Johnston begins peace talks with Federal major general William T. Sherman near Durham Station, North Carolina.

April 18—Battle of Boykin's Mill, south of Camden.

April 19—Potter's men are engaged in skirmishes at Dinkin's Mill and Beech Creek, both north of Stateburg, South Carolina. The latter is the last Civil War encounter in the state where the war started.

April 20—Potter's men destroy the Camden railroad spur.

April 21—Upon receiving word of Lee's surrender, Potter's men march toward Georgetown.

April 22—Potter goes to Hilton Head, South Carolina; command of the division goes to Colonel Brown.

April 25—The raiders arrive in Georgetown.

April 26—Johnson surrenders to Sherman.

Notes

Introduction

1. Mood, "Recollections of Potter's Raid XIX," 1.
2. Edgar, *South Carolina*, 374.

Chapter 1

3. Portions of this chapter previously appeared in pages 382–85 of Elmore, *Carnival of Destruction*.
4. *War of the Rebellion: A Compilation of the Official Records of the Union and Confederate Armies* (henceforth referred to as *Official Records*) 47/2:538, 662. Sherman had had an unsuccessful cavalry raid to free the Union prisoners at the infamous Camp Sumter in Andersonville, Georgia, and a raid into Aiken, South Carolina, was a spectacular failure. See Elmore, *Carnival of Destruction*, for more on the Aiken raid.

   Howard (1830–1909) was an 1854 graduate of West Point who taught mathematics at his alma mater before the war. Though he was brave—he lost an arm at the Battle of Seven Pines, for which he received the Medal of Honor—his war record was at best mediocre. Despite this, he was a corps commander by 1863, and in 1864, he was chosen, amid some controversy, to command the Army of the Tennessee (named for the river, not the state), which he led very capably until the war's end.

A very devout Christian who truly cared about the welfare of slaves and freed blacks, he was the head of the Freedmen's Bureau during Reconstruction. Afterward, he served in the Southwest, was the superintendent of West Point and commanded the Division of the East until he retired from the army in 1894.

Unlike many of his Civil War peers, Howard never spent a day as a civilian from the time he entered West Point until his retirement. He spent his remaining years in Vermont writing about his experiences during and after the war. He also lectured and wrote about religious and education issues. Howard University in Washington, D.C., is named for him.

5. *Official Records* 47/1:202, 255.
6. Ibid., 255.
7. Ibid. Beverly had recently served as part of the Charleston garrison under Lieutenant General William Hardee. Hardee had evacuated Charleston on February 17, 1865. Howard had a chance to capture Hardee's army in Cheraw but delayed his move on the town for so long that Hardee's entire force escaped to North Carolina.
8. Hitchcock, *Marching with Sherman*, 265; *Official Records* 47/1:255.
9. *Official Records* 47/2:142. The 3rd South Carolina Cavalry had been a part of the forces evacuated from Charleston. They were en route to Cheraw but were ordered to go to Florence and join Robertson. Afterward, the regiment was ordered to join Hampton and Butler, which they did outside Greensboro, North Carolina, several weeks later. One of the Federal raiders was architect J.L. Klickner, who designed the Darlington home of Confederate colonel Samuel H. Wilds. When Klickner learned that his creation was to be destroyed, he asked that it be delayed, hoping he could figure out a way to save it. In a bizarre twist of fate, his hopes came true when the unexpected Confederate counterattack denied the Union soldiers the opportunity to burn it.
10. Smith, "Charles Jones Colcock," 32–35, 38. For an excellent history of the Charleston and Savannah Railroad, see H. David Stone Jr.'s *Vital Rails: The Charleston & Savannah Railroad and the Civil War in Coastal South Carolina* (University of South Carolina Press, 2008).
11. Smith, "Charles Jones Colcock," 37. See Elmore, *Carnival of Destruction*, for more on the evacuation of Charleston.
12. Wright, *History of the Sixth Iowa Infantry*, 422; Wills, *Army Life of an Illinois Soldier*, 356–57. The 1941 WPA guide to South Carolina repeats this claim, as does a

monument erected in 1949 by the United Daughters of the Confederacy on the site of the skirmish. However, the latter makes no mention of Williams's orders to destroy the railroads and its equipment. The site of the prison camp is now next to a national cemetery. For more information on the Florence Stockade, see www.nps.gov/Nr/twhp/wwwlps/lessons/142Florence/142FlorenceStockade.htm. The raiders did not reach the prison camp.

13. *Official Records* 47/1:255.
14. Ibid.
15. Ibid.
16. Ibid., 255–56.
17. Ibid., 230.
18. Harwell and Racine, *Fiery Trail*, 168; Wills, *Army Life of an Illinois Soldier*, 358. In his 1908 Memoirs, Howard wrote that he was "chagrin" at the raid's failure and accused the officers of not being "sufficiently vigorous" in its execution. This raises the possibility that he might have influenced Sherman's decision to make a second attempt to get the rail cars.
19. *Official Records* 47/2:721.
20. Ibid., 856.
21. Warner, *Generals in Blue*, 176–77.
22. Ibid.
23. *Official Records* 47/2:856–57. Sumter, South Carolina, was known as Sumterville from its chartering in 1800 until 1855, when it was shortened to Sumter upon the renewal of the town's charter. However, Union troops, for reasons unknown, referred to the town as Sumterville during the raid. (The town was also often misspelled as "Sumpter.") The town was named for Brigadier General Thomas Sumter, a partisan leader during the American Revolution who was known as the Gamecock.
24. Harwell and Racine, *Fiery Trail*, 200.
25. Sherman, *Memoirs*, vol. 2, 299.
26. *Official Records* 47/2:525.
27. Ibid., 533.
28. *Official Records of the Union and Confederate Navies in the War of the Rebellion* (henceforth referred to as *Naval Records*) 16:268, 272; *Official Records* 47/2:575, 615. Shortly after capturing the port on March 1, 1861, Admiral Dahlgren's flagship, the USS *Harvest Moon*, was struck by a Confederate mine and sank in nearby Winyah Bay. Remains of the ship can still be seen at low tide near Battery White at the Belle Isle Yacht Club, just outside Georgetown.
29. *Naval Records* 16:273; Emilio, *History of the Fifty-Fourth Regiment*, 290.

30. Barlow, *Company G*, 217.
31. Ibid. Brigadier General John Porter Hatch (1822–1901) was an 1845 graduate of West Point and a veteran of the Mexican War. After that conflict, he served in the Southwest and was stationed in New Mexico when the war started. He was sent back east, promoted to brigadier general and had an unspectacular career in the field until he was wounded in the leg at the Battle of South Mountain on September 14, 1862, while leading a division. After the battle, he received a Medal of Honor and was promoted to major general for his actions. From that point on, Hatch primarily held administrative positions, eventually becoming head of the District of Charleston by the war's end. He stayed in the army after the war and got caught up in the crazy postwar shuffling of rank, which left him a major in cavalry and returned him to the western frontier, where he served in various forts and engagements. He was promoted to lieutenant colonel in 1873 and full colonel in 1881. He retired in 1886 and spent his remaining years in New York City, where he died. He is buried at Arlington National Cemetery.
32. *Official Records* 47/3:40.
33. Ibid., 81.
34. Ibid., 59.
35. Warner, *Generals in Blue*, 380.
36. Ibid.
37. Emilio, *History of the Fifty-Fourth Regiment*, 290; *Official Records* 47/1:1027.
38. *Official Records* 47/1:1027–28. Biographical information on Brown comes from his obituary published in the April 20, 1881 *Madison Observer*. Regimental history comes from the National Park Service's "Civil War Soldiers and Sailors Database" website: www.nps.gov/civilwar/.htm.
39. *Official Records* 47/1:1027–28; Emilio, *History of the Fifty-Fourth Regiment*, 290. Regimental histories from the National Park Service's "Civil War Soldiers and Sailors Database" website.
40. Biographical information from http://battleofolustee.org//reports/hallowell.htm. See also Emilio, *History of the Fifty-Fourth Regiment*, for Hallowell's tenure as the commander of the 54th Massachusetts.
41. Ibid.
42. *Official Records* 47/1:1027–28; Emilio, *History of the Fifty-Fourth Regiment*, 287, 290. See also http://www.nps.gov/resources/story.htm?id=210. While the term "colored" is now archaic, I have chosen to use it here, as that was part of the regiments' names. Likewise, unless otherwise noted, all spelling and grammar are original.
43. Regimental histories from the National Park Service's "Civil War Soldiers and Sailors Database" website.

44. Ibid; Phisterer, *New York in the War of the Rebellion*, 335; *Official Records* 47/1:1041.
45. See www.archives.gov/education/lessons/blacks-civil-war. Based on period writings, it seems that many South Carolinians saw the use of black troops as a deliberate insult to the state.

CHAPTER 2

46. *Official Records* 47/1:1027; Emilio, *History of the Fifty-Fourth Regiment*, 290; *Official Records* 47/3:98; Moore, "Last Officer," 3.
47. *Official Records* 47/1:98, 1028.
48. *Official Records* 47/3:126.
49. Ibid. Hartwell was a general only by brevet or honorary rank, given in recognition for his gallant conduct at the Battle of Honey Hill (South Carolina) on November 30, 1864. After the war, he served as a justice on the Supreme Court of Hawaii under both Royal Hawaiian rule and U.S. territorial rule.
50. *Official Records* 47/3:148–49.
51. *Official Records* 47/1:1028; Emilio, *History of the Fifty-Fourth Regiment*, 291.
52. Ibid; McGill, *Narrative of Reminiscences*, 219; Moore, "Last Officer," 3; Culp, *25th Ohio Vet. Volunteer Infantry*, 121–22; Barlow, *Company G*, 219.
53. The son of an Irish immigrant, Andre Gordon Magrath (1813–1893) was a Harvard-trained lawyer and a district court judge for both the U.S. and Confederate States governments. He also signed the Ordinance of Secession. A strong advocate of states' rights, Magrath often clashed with Davis and ruled against many of his policies. Some believe that Magrath ran for governor out of fear of losing his judgeship. Magrath was elected on December 14, 1864, and sworn in five days later. He would spend much of his short term as governor trying—and failing—to find ways to defend South Carolina from Sherman.

    When Sherman occupied the state capital, Columbia, on February 17, 1865, Magrath fled the city. He tried to reconvene the state legislature in Greenville on April 25, but due to a lack of a quorum, he could only brief those in attendance on the situation at hand. Orders for his arrest on the charge of treason forced him to resign as governor on May 22. Three days later, Magrath surrendered himself to Federal authorities. After being briefly imprisoned, he returned to his hometown of Charleston, where he enjoyed a successful law practice. For more on Governor Magrath's life and his role as governor, see Williamson, "The Disruption of State Government in South Carolina."

54. Andrew G. Magrath's Papers—Letters Received and Sent Dec. 21, 1864–April 25, 1865; Seigler, *South Carolina's Military Organizations*, 225, 245; Boddie, *History of Williamsburg*, 429.
55. Boddie, *History of Williamsburg*, 429; Harwell and Racine, *Fiery Trail*, 200; Ramsey, "Farewell Shot," 8. Ramsey served in Garden's Company, South Carolina Light Artillery, also known as the Palmetto Light Battery, and had seen action in Longstreet's Corps in the Army of Northern Virginia.
56. Boddie, *History of Williamsburg*, 430–31; McGill, *Narrative of Reminiscences*, 220; *Official Records* 47/1:1028.
57. Steele in *Our Women in the War*, 320.
58. Emilio, *History of the Fifty-Fourth Regiment*, 291; Steele in *Our Women in the War*, 320.
59. Steele in *Our Women in the War*, 320.
60. Ibid.
61. *Official Records* 47/1:1028.
62. *Official Records* 47/3:126.
63. Emilio, *History of the Fifty-Fourth Regiment*, 292.
64. Ibid., 292–93; Moore, "Last Officer," 4.
65. Mood, "Recollections of Potter's Raid II," 2.
66. Ibid.
67. Marszalek, *Diary of Miss Emma Holmes*, 432.
68. Culp, *25th Ohio Vet. Volunteer Infantry*, 122; Barlow, *Company G*, 219.
69. Mood, "Recollections of Potter's Raid II," 2.
70. Ibid.; Mood, "Recollections of Potter's Raid III," 2.
71. Ibid.; Boddie, *History of Williamsburg*, 429; National Park Service, "Civil War Soldiers and Sailors Database."
72. *Official Records* 47/1:1028.
73. Emilio, *History of the Fifty-Fourth Regiment*, 293; Moore, "Last Officer," 6.
74. Moore, "Last Officer," 4.
75. Mood, "Recollections of Potter's Raid III," 2; Thigpen, *Illustrated Recollections of Potter's Raid*, 69.
76. Mood, "Recollections of Potter's Raid III," 2.
77. Emilio, *History of the Fifty-Fourth Regiment*, 293; *Official Records* 47/1:1028; Mood, "Recollections of Potter's Raid VI," 2.
78. Mood, "Recollections of Potter's Raid VI," 2.
79. Ibid.
80. Graham, "How Charley H. Jones Killed a Yankee Soldier," 3.

81. Ibid. Allegedly, there was a price put on Jones's head by the Federals. After the war, Lieutenant Jones became the sheriff of Sumter County.
82. *Official Records* 47/1:1028; Emilio, *History of the Fifty-Fourth Regiment*, 293.
83. Culp, *25th Ohio Vet. Volunteer Infantry*, 122–23; Emilio, *History of the Fifty-Fourth Regiment*, 293; Mood, "Recollections of Potter's Raid IX," 1; M.R.R. in *Our Women in the War*. Culp claimed that an unfinished edition of the *Clarion Banner* was waiting to be printed when the Federals arrived. Allegedly, the paper called for the assassination of Potter, but this claim is not substantiated by anyone else.
84. Emilio, *History of the Fifty-Fourth Regiment*, 293.
85. *Clarendon Banner of Freedom*, April 9, 1865, 1.
86. Ibid.
87. Mood, "Recollections of Potter's Raid X," 2, and "Recollections of Potter's Raid XI," 1.
88. Mood, "Recollections of Potter's Raid XI," 1.
89. Ibid.
90. Ibid.
91. Ibid.; *Clarendon Banner of Freedom*, April 9, 1865, 1. House slaves were often referred to as "servants," but it is unclear if the Moods had a slave or really had a paid servant.
92. M.R.R. in *Our Women in the War*, 293; Clark, *Clarendon Local Confederate History*, 343; Moore, "Last Officer," 6.
93. M.R.R. in *Our Women in the War*, 294; Moore, "Last Officer," 7; Emilio, *History of the Fifty-Fourth Regiment*, 294.
94. Moore, "Last Officer," 6.

Chapter 3

95. Emilio, *History of the Fifty-Fourth Regiment*, 294; Barlow, *Company G*, 219.
96. Mood, "Recollections of Potter's Raid VII," 1.
97. Ibid.; Garland, "Battle of Dingle's Mill," 549; *Official Records* 47/1:1028.
98. Warner, *Generals in Gray*, 185–86. The brigade's nickname came from how the Confederacy viewed the soldiers as "orphans." Though represented in the Confederate Congress, Kentucky never fully seceded from the Union and thus was in a state of limbo. The term probably gained popularity after the war. The Whig Party evolved into the Republican Party in the 1850s.

Jones's military status at this point in the war is confusing and mysterious. He had been elected as lieutenant in Company I of the 7th South Carolina Cavalry in August 1864, but his superior officer, Alexander Cheves Haskell, refused to allow him to take his position. Jones did assume it in February 1865, when Haskell went on medical leave. Upon his return, Jones asked for a transfer. When it was denied, Jones tendered his resignation in March 1865, a month before Potter's raid. While there is evidence that Jones might have been brought up on court-martial charges, it is also possible that he was promoted on March 16, 1865. It is also unknown why he was in South Carolina while his regiment was with Lee in Virginia.

Adding to the mystery is that some accounts list Jones as a captain and others as a lieutenant. Since we can verify the latter, I have chosen to refer to him by that rank. See Terrar, "Family History Information About Charles H. Jones and Elizabeth Margaret David Jones."

99. Mood, "Recollections of Potter's Raid VII," 1.

100. M.R.R. in *Our Women in the War*, 290, 294; Gregorie, *History of Sumter County*, 291.

101. Ibid.; National Parks Service, "Civil War Soldiers and Sailors Database." The 1860 census listed the population of the Sumter District at 23,859.

102. M.R.R. in *Our Women in the War*, 290, 294; Gregorie, *History of Sumter County*, 262.

103. Garland, "Battle of Dingle's Mill," 549. The spelling of Lieutenant Painpare's name varies in the different accounts of the battle. Local historians believe that the spelling presented here is the correct one.

Lieutenant McQueen had started the war as a member of the Palmetto Light Artillery and had seen action at the Battles of Sharpsburg and the Crater. In the latter, he personally fired mortar rounds at the advancing Federal forces to try to stop their advance. On the third day of the Battle of Gettysburg, McQueen and his artillery team were involved in Pickett's Charge with only one field Howitzer. Despite being fired at by twenty Union artillery pieces, he and his men stood their ground. During the bombardment, McQueen's team lost four men and six horses, with the lieutenant being severely wounded in the head.

McQueen returned to duty, only to be wounded again outside Richmond, Virginia, on October 7, 1864. He was sent home to Sumter and was recovering from this injury when Potter's men arrived.

104. Gregorie, *History of Sumter County*, 262; Ramsey, "Farewell Shot," 8; Garland, "Battle of Dingle's Mill," 549. The millpond no longer exists.

105. Garland, "Battle of Dingle's Mill," 549.

106. Ibid., 262; Ramsey, "Farewell Shot," 8.
107. Gregorie, *History of Sumter County*, 262.
108. Andrews, *Life and Adventures*, 46, 49; McLaurin, "Narrative of the War," 46; Thigpen, *Illustrated Recollections of Potter's Raid*. Captain Andres served with the 22nd South Carolina Artillery.
109. Moore, "Last Officer," 7; Emilio, *History of the Fifty-Fourth Regiment*, 294; *Official Records* 47/1:1026, 1028; Garland, "Battle of Dingle's Mill," 549. There was a failed attempt to fire Sergeant Dunbar's gun without the primer.
110. Garland, "Battle of Dingle's Mill," 549; *Official Records* 47/1:1028; Gregorie, *History of Sumter County*, 262; Beyer and Keydel, *Deeds of Valor*, 494–96.
111. Beyer and Keydel, *Deeds of Valor*, 496.
112. *Official Records* 47/1:1028; Gregorie, *History of Sumter County*, 262.
113. Ramsey, "Farewell Shot," 8; Gregorie, *History of Sumter County*, 262.
114. Garland, "Battle of Dingle's Mill," 549; Ramsey, "Farewell Shot," 8; *Official Records* 47/1:1041. Two more rounds were fired after the battle near the town of Sumter.
115. *Official Records* 47/1:1028. Carmichael (1829–1889) is listed in the 1860 census as a cabinet manufacturer and is listed in an obituary as president of the Crown Manufacturing Company of Phelps, New York. He became a major when the regiment was organized in 1862. He was promoted to lieutenant colonel in 1863 and full colonel in 1865. He was discharged from the army with the rest of the regiment on July 10, 1865, in Charleston, South Carolina. He returned to manufacturing after the war and was active in local politics. At the time of his death, he had been an invalid for a year. Forty former members of his regiment attended his funeral.
116. Barlow, *Company G*, 220.
117. Ramsey, "Farewell Shot," 8.
118. Ibid.; Gregorie, *History of Sumter County*, 262; Barlow, *Company G*, 220.
119. *Official Records* 47/1:1026, 1029; Gregorie, *History of Sumter County*, 264; Culp, *25th Vet. Volunteer Infantry*, 125; Thigpen, *Illustrated Recollections of Potter's Raid*, 269. The Confederate casualty figures comes from a report by Colonel George W. Lee that appeared in the April 4, 1913 edition of the *Sumter Herald*. However, it does not appear in the *Official Records*, which makes it suspect.
120. Barlow, *Company G*, 222.
121. *Official Records* 47/1:1031. Chipman (1823–1910) was a West Point graduate and a career military man. Originally an officer of the 2nd Michigan Infantry, he saw action at Chancellorsville and Gettysburg. He

assumed command of the 102nd U.S. Colored Troops in 1864 with the rank of full colonel. He was brevetted to brigadier general in March 1865. After the war, he was a major in the 3rd U.S. Infantry. He retired from the army in 1887. He died and was buried in Detroit. Like all officers in Potter's black regiments, he was white.

122. "Commendation by Col. P.P. Brown, Jr. April 12, 1865, from Singleton Plantation, S.C." reprinted in Helm, *History of Wabash County*, 291. The citation does not appear in the *Official Records*, though Helm claimed that Finkenbiner kept a copy.
123. Gregorie, *History of Sumter County*, 264.
124. Ibid.; Marszalek, *Diary of Miss Emma Holmes*, 432.
125. Gregorie, *History of Sumter County*, 264; Culp, *25th Vet. Volunteer Infantry*, 125; Emilio, *History of the Fifty-Fourth Regiment*, 295; Moore, "Last Officer," 8.
126. Gregorie, *History of Sumter County*, 264, 265.
127. Ibid., 265; Moore, "Last Officer," 8–9; Barlow, *Company G*, 225–26.
128. Andrews, *Life and Adventures*, 49.
129. Ibid., 49–54. Andrews served as Sumter's police chief immediately after the war.
130. Gregorie, *History of Sumter County*, 265.
131. Ibid.
132. Haynesworth, *Haynesworth-Furman and Allied Families*, 97–98.
133. McLaurin, "Narrative of the War," 461.
134. Marszalek, *Diary of Miss Emma Holmes*, 434.
135. Emilio, *History of the Fifty-Fourth Regiment*, 295; Barlow, *Company G*, 226. Emilio claimed thirteen guns were fired, while Barlow says it was fifteen.
136. Barlow, *Company G*, 222–24.
137. Ibid., 224. According to the Bible, Samson slew an entire army using only the jawbone of a donkey.
138. Gregorie, *History of Sumter County*, 265; *Official Records* 47/1:1026, 1029.
139. *Official Records* 47/3:785. John C. Breckenridge had been vice president under James Buchannan from 1857 to 1861 and was the Southern Democrats' presidential candidate in 1860. Though a sitting U.S. senator from Kentucky and an opponent of secession, an arrest warrant was issued for him, turning him to the Confederate side, where he served as a general and, in 1865, as secretary of war. Lee considered him the best of all the Confederate war secretaries.
140. *Official Records* 47/3:162.
141. Ibid.
142. Moore, "Last Officer," 8.

143. Gregorie, *History of Sumter County*, 266; Marszalek, *Diary of Miss Emma Holmes*, 434; Culp, *25th Ohio Vet. Volunteer Infantry*, 125–26.

144. Marszalek, *Diary of Miss Emma Holmes*, 434.

145. Barlow, *Company G*, 226.

146. Ibid.

147. Culp, *25th Ohio Vet. Volunteer Infantry*, 126.

148. Gregorie, *History of Sumter County*, 266.

149. *Official Records* 47/3:162; Gregorie, *History of Sumter County*, 265; Mood, "Recollections of Potter's Raid XIX," 1. Mayesville was a prosperous farming community until it was bypassed by a highway leading into Sumter in the 1920s. Its decline was accelerated by the Great Depression. Today, it is almost a ghost town.

150. Gregorie, *History of Sumter County*, 68–70. The town was abandoned in 1872, when the railroad moved its route to the nearby town of Wedgefield.

151. Barlow, *Company G*, 226

152. Sumter, *Stateburg and Its People*, 36, 53; Culp, *25th Ohio Vet. Volunteer Infantry*, 127; Gregorie, *History of Sumter County*, 266; Emilio, *History of the Fifty-Fourth Regiment*, 298; Moore, "Last Officer," 10. This author has doubts about this tale, as Potter would have surely known that if he killed a prisoner, the Confederates would most likely kill several of their prisoners in retaliation. Midway burned down in the 1930s, allegedly due to a drunken overseer.

153. Sumter, *Stateburg and Its People*, 54.

154. Ibid.

155. Ibid.

156. Emilio, *History of the Fifty-Fourth Regiment*, 296.

157. Ibid. Swails was a free light-skinned African American and might have been the Union army's first black officer. After the war, he became a lawyer and returned to South Carolina to enjoy a successful political career during Reconstruction. Welch would end the war as a lieutenant.

158. Ibid.

159. Ibid., 297; Moore, "Last Officer," 10.

160. Emilio, *History of the Fifty-Fourth Regiment*, 297.

161. Ibid., 297–98. There is no record of Swails, who was a waiter before the war, having ever worked on a train; in fact, he claimed he was boatman on his enlistment papers.

162. Ibid., 298.

163. Ibid.; Moore, "Last Officer," 10. The plantation no longer exists and is marked by a granite monument located in a mobile home community.

164. *Official Records* 47/1:1,029. Lieutenant Stevens claimed that there were forty-eight cars. In a subsequent report filed on April 26, Potter claimed forty-five cars were destroyed.
165. Ibid., 1,026, 1,029. Several accounts claim that the number of slaves sent back was in the thousands.
166. Emilio, *History of the Fifty-Fourth Regiment*, 298; Moore, "Last Officer," 10. Wright's Bluff was the site of two major skirmishes during the American Revolution.
167. McLaurin, "Narrative of the War," 468.
168. Marszalek, *Diary of Miss Emma Holmes*, 434.
169. Ibid.
170. *Official Records* 47/3:117. The 55th Massachusetts was a "colored regiment," while the 54th New York was predominately German.
171. Ibid.
172. Ibid., 126.
173. Ibid., 138.
174. Ibid., 177.
175. *Official Records* 47/1:1,040. Chipman's report misspells Stateburg, which has only one "s."
176. Ibid.
177. Moore, "Last Officer," 10.
178. Emilio, *History of the Fifty-Fourth Regiment*, 299.
179. Ibid.
180. Ibid.; Culp, *25th Ohio Vet. Volunteer Infantry*, 12; Barlow, *Company G*, 227–28; *Official Records* 47/3:1,026.
181. Gregorie, *History of Sumter County*, 268; *Official Records* 47/3:333.
182. Emilio, *History of the Fifty-Fourth Regiment*, 299–300.
183. Gregorie, *History of Sumter County*, 268.
184. Ibid.; Kirkland and Kennedy, *Historic Camden, Part 2*, 174; Culp, *25th Ohio Vet. Volunteer Infantry*, 129.
185. "Old Cannon at Bishopville, S.C.," 211. The cannon lay there until 1867, when it was hauled to Bishopville. It was fired in 1876 to celebrate former Confederate general Wade Hampton III's election as governor, effectively ending Reconstruction in South Carolina. It was fired again in 1902 to celebrate Lee County's founding.
186. *Official Records* 47/3: 236. Halleck received the message on the twentieth.
187. Ibid., 237, 1026. Sherman's message was delivered by courier.
188. Ibid., 1,026; Gregorie, *History of Sumter County*, 268; Emilio, *History of the Fifty-Fourth Regiment*, 300; Moore, "Last Officer," 10; Barlow, *Company G*,

228–29. The tune for "John Brown's Body" is better known today as "The Battle Hymn of the Republic."

189. Gregorie, *History of Sumter County*, 268; Emilio, *History of the Fifty-Fourth Regiment*, 300; Moore, "Last Officer," 10. For more on Sherman's raid on Camden, see Elmore, *Carnival of Destruction*, 340–44.

190. Kirkland and Kennedy, *Historic Camden, Part 2*, 174.

CHAPTER 4

191. Emilio, *History of the Fifty-Fourth Regiment*, 300; Barlow, *Company G*, 229; Kirkland and Kennedy, *Historic Camden, Part 2*, 174. Hannon's Brigade was named after its former commander, Moses Wright Hannon (1827–1897). Hannon was probably not in South Carolina at this time, as he had been wounded at the Battle of Monroe's Crossroads in North Carolina, which ended his field service to the Confederacy. Though he was appointed an acting brigadier general in 1864, there is no record of him ever being permanently promoted to that rank.

192. Emilio, *History of the Fifty-Fourth Regiment*, 300.

193. Biographical information on General Young comes from Holland, *Pierce M.B. Young*, 348; Gregorie, *History of Sumter County*, 348.

194. Emilio, *History of the Fifty-Fourth Regiment*, 300–01; Kirkland and Kennedy, *Historic Camden, Part 2*, 174; Boykin, *Captain Alexander Hamilton Boykin*, 181.

195. Boykin, *Captain Alexander Hamilton Boykin*, 184.

196. Emilio, *History of the Fifty-Fourth Regiment*, 301.

197. Moore, "The Last Officer," 2; Emilio, *History of the Fifty-Fourth Regiment*, 303; Boykin, *Captain Alexander Hamilton Boykin*, 185. The body was originally buried at the battle site.

198. http://www.fas.harvard.edu/~memhall/names.html; Boykin, *Captain Alexander Hamilton Boykin*, 185. Stevens is on plaque number seventeen; he was one of eight men from Harvard's class of 1863 to die in the war.

199. Emilio, *History of the Fifty-Fourth Regiment*, 303–04.

200. Boykin, *Captain Alexander Hamilton Boykin*, 185.

201. Emilio, *History of the Fifty-Fourth Regiment*, 300–01; *Official Records* 47/1:1,026.

202. *Official Records* 47/1:1,029–30.

203. Emilio, *History of the Fifty-Fourth Regiment*, 304.

204. Ibid.; *Official Records* 47/3:1,026.

205. Gregorie, *History of Sumter County*, 269; Barlow, *Company G*, 229; *Official Records* 47/1:1,030.

206. *Official Records* 47/1:1,040.
207. Emilio, *History of the Fifty-Fourth Regiment*, 305; Barlow, *Company G*, 230; *Official Records* 47/3:1,026. Some accounts state that the 102nd Colored Troops participated in this encounter as well.
208. *Official Records* 47/1:1,030.
209. Ibid., 1,026; Gregorie, *History of Sumter County*, 269; Emilio, *History of the Fifty-Fourth Regiment*, 305; Kirkland and Kennedy, *Historic Camden, Part 2*, 174.
210. *Official Records* 47/1:1,026, 1,030–31. The "Stateburg" name comes from an unsuccessful attempt by local landowners, including Revolutionary War hero General Thomas Sumter, to have South Carolina move its state capital to this site after the Revolution.
211. www.lat34north.com/HistoricMarkersSC/CountyDetail.cfm?CountyNameKey=Sumter.
212. Culp, *25th Ohio Vet. Volunteer Infantry Regiment*, 132; Barlow, *Company G*, 231; *Official Records* 47/3:1,026, 1031. Some of the shrapnel from the 1865 explosions still remained and was collected for scrap metal during World War II. For an interesting account of a 1997 visit to the now-abandoned site, see http://library.sc.edu/socar/uscs/newslt97/safari.html.
213. Emilio, *History of the Fifty-Fourth Regiment*, 306.
214. Ibid.
215. *Official Records* 47/3:274.
216. Ibid.
217. Gregorie, *History of Sumter County*, 269.
218. Ibid., 270.
219. Ibid.
220. Ibid. A popular legend states that the architect of the house was General Potter's brother. However, the architect is unknown. Nathaniel F. Potter was the home's builder, but since he came from Rhode Island and the general came from New York, and since there is no mention of a brother in General Potter's obituary, this claim is questionable.
221. Ibid.
222. Ibid., 270–71.
223. Ibid.
224. Emilio, *History of the Fifty-Fourth Regiment*, 307; Holland, *Pierce M.B. Young*, 104. Holland claimed that he surrendered to Potter on April 22, 1865, but Potter makes no mention of this in his reports.
225. Culp, *25th Ohio Vet. Volunteer Infantry Regiment*, 133.
226. Gregorie, *History of Sumter County*, 271.

227. Ibid.; Barlow, *Company G*, 231.
228. *Official Records* 47/1:1,026, 1,031.
229. Barlow, *Company G*, 231–32.
230. *Official Records* 47/3:274.
231. Emilio, *History of the Fifty-Fourth Regiment*, 307–08.
232. Ibid., 308; Culp, *25th Ohio Vet. Volunteer Infantry Regiment*, 133; Barlow, *Company G*, 232; *Official Records* 47/3:1,031.
233. Emilio, *History of the Fifty-Fourth Regiment*, 308; Barlow, *Company G*, 232.
234. Emilio, *History of the Fifty-Fourth Regiment*, 308.
235. Ibid.; Barlow, *Company G*, 233.
236. Barlow, *Company G*, 233–34.
237. Ibid., 234; *Emilio, History of the Fifty-Fourth Regiment*, 308.
238. *Official Records* 47/3:1,027.
239. Ibid.
240. Ibid.
241. Emilio, *History of the Fifty-Fourth Regiment*, 308–09; Barlow, *Company G*, 235.
242. Barlow, *Company G*, 235. Barlow puts the number of slaves who followed the raiders at three thousand, as opposed to Potter's estimate of five thousand.
243. Ibid., 235–36.
244. *Official Records* 47/3:318.

CHAPTER 5

245. Ibid., 333.
246. Ibid., 242. Gilmore also passed this suggestion along to Edwin Stanton, the U.S. secretary of war.
247. *Official Records* 47/3:274; 46/2:414; 47/1:19–20.
248. *Official Records* 47/3:255, 359.
249. Ibid., 525, 453. Brigadier General John P. Hatch would end up being sent to Orangeburg.
250. Emilio, *History of the Fifty-Fourth Regiment*, 310.
251. *Official Records* 47/1:1,026.
252. Ibid. Brevet or honorary promotions were used by the Union army to honor gallantry in combat or fill specific needs in a military unit's command structure. In the case of the latter, which happened mostly in the early days of the war, the soldier might be paid at the brevet rank, which was often higher than his actual rank. They were also awarded very

early in the war to many West Point graduates because Congress limited the number of officer commissions the army could give, and there were no open commissions. During the war, all brevet officers were allowed to wear the insignia of and be referred to by their brevet rank.

Because Union army officers often held commissions in both the regular army and the U.S. Volunteers during the war, an officer could hold four different commissions. An example of this is George Armstrong Custer, who was a commissioned major general in the U.S. Volunteers and held brevets as a major general in both the volunteers and the regular army but whose regular army rank was only lieutenant colonel.

About 1,700 officers received brevets for brigadier and/or major general in both U.S. armies. When the Civil War ended, the U.S. Volunteers were disbanded, making any rank held in that body null and void, resulting in a number of generals, like Custer, becoming junior officers. The army spent years after the war trying to determine the proper rank and insignia for many of these men.

Though Confederate army regulations allowed for brevet promotions, none are believed to have been issued. The last U.S. Army brevet was issued in 1918.

253. Ibid., 1,026–27.
254. Woodward, *Mary Chesnut's Civil War*, 803.
255. "Letter from B. Hood, Sumter, S.C., to Relatives in the North, August 24, 1865."
256. Warner, *Generals in Blue*, 380–81; *New York Times*, "Funeral of Gen. Potter," June 5, 1889.
257. Barlow, *Company G*, 236; *Madison Observer*, April 20, 1881; Ancestry.com.
258. Biographical information from FindaGrave.com and Wikipedia.
259. Ibid.; Warner, *Generals in Blue*, 177.
260. Smith, "Charles Jones Colcock," 38–39.
261. Warner, *Generals in Gray*, 348; Holland, *Pierce M.B. Young*.
262. http://www.history.army.mil/html/moh/civwaral.html. Barrell (1842–1914) was originally from Michigan. After the war, he returned to Michigan, where he held various jobs prior to his death. He is buried in Wayland, Michigan.
263. http://www.history.army.mil/moh/civilwar. Finkenbiner (1842–1822) was described as an "industrious famer." He had been wounded on Cemetery Hill during the Battle of Gettysburg. He is buried in Lagro, Indiana.
264. http://scscv.com/confederate-past-and-present/confederate-medal-of-honor-recipients. Lieutenant William McQueen, who was killed at

the Battle of Dingle's Mill, has also been so honored by the Sons of Confederate Veterans for his actions at the Battle of Gettysburg.

265. Ibid.

CHAPTER 6

266. Barlow, *Company G*, 234–35.

267. Ibid., 235.

268. Sherman, *Memoirs*, 299. On April 10, Sherman reported his combined forces at 89,948 men, but this figure includes the 26,392-man Army of the Ohio, which joined him later. This means that Sherman had over 63,000 men to face Johnston.

269. It is worth noting that Sherman did let slide a failed raid on Aiken, South Carolina, but the idea for that raid was imitated by his cavalry commander and was given, at best, only lukewarm support by Sherman. Florence, on the other hand, was an idea on which Sherman totally signed off. See Elmore, *Carnival of Destruction*, 136–45, for more on the Aiken raid. After the war, Sherman gave up to a third of his income to help veterans in need.

270. Figures taken from eighth U.S. census. Broken down, the county populations were Clarendon, 13,095; Georgetown, 21,305; Kershaw, 13,086; Sumter, 23,859; and Williamsburg, 15,489. It should be noted that the skirmish at Spring Hill took place in what is now Lee County; however, in 1865, it was still a part of Sumter County.

271. There was a United Confederate Veterans Camp in Cartersville, Georgia, northwest of Atlanta, that was named for General Young, and the current United Daughters of the Confederacy Chapter in Cartersville is named after him.

272. Boddie, *History of Williamsburg*, 429.

273. Seigler, *Guide to Confederate Monuments in South Carolina*, 483–85. The park contains memorial graves to three Union soldiers who died at the battle and are buried somewhere in the park in a common grave. There is also a more recent memorial to the Confederate casualties of the battle.

274. South Carolina Highway Historical Marker Guide, 133, 144, 223–24.

275. Ibid., 229; www.lat34north.com/HistoricMarkersSC/CountyDetail.cfm?CountyNameKey=Sumter.

276. Seigler, *Guide to Confederate Monuments in South Carolina*, 85–88. A recent visit to the monument found it mostly covered up by shrubbery.

277. Thigpen, *Illustrated Recollections of Potter's Raid*. The book is currently out of print.
278. www.lat34north.com/HistoricMarkersSC/CountyDetail.cfm?CountyNameKey=Sumter; Sumter, South Carolina Last Days: *Potter's Raid & the Civil War* (brochure produced by the Sumter Convention and Visitors Bureau, Sumter, SC).
279. Kirkland and Kennedy, *Historic Camden, Part 2*, 174–75. The letter was dated April 24, 1865.

Bibliography

Primary Sources

Barlow, Albert Rowe. *Company G: A Record of the Services of One Company of the 157th N.Y. Vols. in the War of the Rebellion, from Sept. 19, 1862, to July 10, 1865, including the Roster of the Company 1899*. Syracuse, NY: A.W. Hall, 1899.

Charleston News and Courier. *"Our Women in the War": The Lives They Lived; The Deaths They Died*. Charleston, SC: News and Courier Book Press, 1885.

Clark, Mrs. Samuel J. *Clarendon Local Confederate History: Recollections and Reminiscences, 1861–1865*. N.p.: United Daughters of the Confederacy, South Carolina Division, 1997.

Culp, Edward C. *The 25th Ohio Vet. Volunteer Infantry in the War for the Union*. Topeka, KS: G.W. Crane & Company, 1885.

Emilio, Luis F. *History of the Fifty-Fourth Regiment of Massachusetts Volunteer Infantry*. Boston: Boston Book Company, 1894.

Garland, W.H. "The Battle of Dingle's Mill." *Confederate Veteran* XXIV, no. 12 (December 1916).

Graham, Daniel J. "How Charley H. Jones Killed a Yankee Soldier and Defied His Pursuers." (Sumter, SC) *Watchman and Southron* 11, no. 8 (September 23, 1891).

Harwell, Richard, and Philip N. Racine, eds. *The Fiery Trail: A Union Officer's Account of Sherman's Last Campaign*. Knoxville: University of Tennessee Press, 1986.

Hitchcock, Henry. *Marching with Sherman*. Lincoln: University of Nebraska Press, 1995.

Howard, Oliver Otis. *Autobiography of Oliver Otis Howard, Major General, United States Army*. Vol. II. New York: Bake and Taylor Company, 1908.

Kirkland, Thomas J., and Robert M. Kennedy. *Historic Camden, Part 2*. Columbia, SC: The State Company, 1926.

"A Letter from B. Hood, Sumter S.C., to Relatives in the North, August 24, 1865." Manuscript Collection, South Caroliniana Library, University of South Carolina, Columbia, SC.

Marszalek, John F., ed. *The Diary of Miss Emma Holmes, 1861–1866*. Baton Rouge: Louisiana State University Press, 1979.

McGill, Samuel D., MD. *Narrative of Reminiscences in Williamsburg County*. Kingstree, SC: Kingstree Lithographic Company, 1894.

McLaurin, Catherine Louisa. "A Narrative of the War." Manuscript located in the archives of the Sumter (SC) County Museum and Archives.

Mood, Reverend William W. "Recollections of Potter's Raid II." (Sumter, SC) *Watchman and Southron* 5, no. 50 (July 13, 1886).

———. "Recollections of Potter's Raid III." (Sumter, SC) *Watchman and Southron* 5, no. 51 (July 20, 1886).

———. "Recollections of Potter's Raid VI." (Sumter, SC) *Watchman and Southron* 6, no. 3 (August 17, 1886).

———. "Recollections of Potter's Raid VII." (Sumter, SC) *Watchman and Southron* 6, no. 5 (August 31, 1886).

———. "Recollections of Potter's Raid IX." (Sumter, SC) *Watchman and Southron* 6, no. 6 (September 7, 1886).

———. "Recollections of Potter's Raid X." (Sumter, SC) *Watchman and Southron* 6, no. 7 (September 14, 1886).

———. "Recollections of Potter's Raid XI." (Sumter, SC) *Watchman and Southron* 6, no. 8 (September 21, 1886).

———. "Recollections of Potter's Raid XIX." (Sumter, SC) *Watchman and Southron* 6, no. 16 (November 16, 1886).

Moore, John Hammond, ed. "The Last Officer—April 1865." *South Carolina Historical Magazine* 67, no. 1 (January 1966).

"The Old Cannon at Bishopville, S.C." *Confederate Veteran* XXVII, no. 6 (June 1919).

Ramsey, James Graves. "A Farewell Shot: The Battle of Dingle's Mill, South Carolina: The Last Days of the Confederacy." (Sumter, SC) *Watchman and Southron* 30, no. 16 (October, 20, 1909).

Sherman, William T. *Memoirs of General William T. Sherman*. 2 vols. New York: Da Capo Press, 1984.

Smith, Gustavus W. "Charles Jones Colcock: A Typical Citizen and Soldier of the Old Regime." *Southern Historical Society Papers* 26 (January–December 1898).

Sumter, Thomas S. *Stateburg and Its People*. 3rd ed. Columbia, SC: State Printing Company, 1982.

Wills, Charles. *Army Life of an Illinois Soldier: Letters and Diary of Charles W. Wills*. Carbondale: Southern Illinois University Press, 1996.

Woodward, C. Vann, ed. *Mary Chesnut's Civil War*. New Haven, CT: Yale University Press, 1981.

Wright, Henry H. *A History of the Sixth Iowa Infantry*. Iowa City: State Historical Society of Iowa, 1923.

OFFICIAL SOURCES

"Commendation by Col. P.P. Brown Jr., April 12, 1865, from Singleton Plantation, S.C." Reprinted in Helm, Thomas B. *History of Wabash County, Indiana*. Chicago: J. Morris, 1884.

Dyer, Frederick H. *A Compendium of the War of the Rebellion*. Des Moines, IA: Dyer Publishing Company, 1908.

Magrath, Governor Andrew Gordon. Andrew G. Magrath's Papers—Letters Received and Sent Dec. 21, 1864–April 25, 1865. South Carolina Department of Archives and History Collection, Columbia, SC.

Official Records of the Union and Confederate Navies in the War of the Rebellion. Washington, D.C.: U.S. Government Printing Office, 1894.

Seigler, Robert S. *A Guide to Confederate Monuments in South Carolina*. Columbia: South Carolina Department of Archives and History, 1997.Columbia, S.C.

South Carolina Highway Historical Marker Guide. Columbia: South Carolina Department of Archives and History, 1998.

War of the Rebellion: A Compilation of the Official Records of the Union and Confederate Armies. 128 vols. Washington, D.C.: U.S. Government Printing Office, 1880–1901.

SECONDARY SOURCES

Andrews, Robert W. *Life and Adventures of Capt. Robert W. Andrews, of Sumter, South Carolina*. Boston: E.P. Whitcomb, 1887.

Beyer, Walter F., and Oscar F. Keydel. *Deeds of Valor: From Records in the Archives of the United States Government; How American Heroes Won the Medal of Honor*. Vol. 1. Detroit: Perrien-Keydel Company, 1907.

Boddie, William Willis. *History of Williamsburg*. Columbia, SC: The State Company, 1923.

Boykin, Richard Manning. *Captain Alexander Hamilton Boykin: One of South Carolina's Distinguished Citizens*. New York: privately published, 1942.

Edgar, Dr. Walter B. *South Carolina: A History*. Columbia: University of South Carolina Press, 1998.

Elmore, Tom. *A Carnival of Destruction: Sherman's Invasion of South Carolina*. Charleston, SC: Joggling Board Press, 2012.

Faust, Patricia L., ed. *Historical Times Illustrated Encyclopedia of the Civil War*. New York: HarperPernnial, 1991.

Gregorie, Anne King. *History of Sumter County*. Sumter, SC: Library Board of Sumter County, 1954.

Haynesworth, Hugh Charles. *Haynesworth-Furman and Allied Families*. Sumter, SC: Osteen Publishing Co., 1942.

Holland, Lynwood M. *Pierce M.B. Young: The Warwick of the South*. Athens: University of Georgia Press, 1964.

Phisterer, Frederick. *New York in the War of the Rebellion, 1861–1865*. 3rd ed. Albany, NY: J.B. Lyon Company, 1912.

Seigler, Robert S. *South Carolina's Military Organizations During the War Between the States: Statewide Units, Militia and Reserves*. Charleston, SC: The History Press, 2008.

Thigpin, Alan D. *The Illustrated Recollections of Potter's Raid, April 5–21, 1865*. Sumter, SC: Gamecock City Printing Inc., 1998.

Warner, Ezra J. *Generals in Blue: Lives of the Union Commanders*. Baton Rouge: Louisiana State University Press, 1964.

———. *Generals in Gray: Lives of the Confederate Commanders*. Baton Rouge: Louisiana State University Press, 1959.

Williamson, Joel R. "The Disruption of State Government in South Carolina During the Magrath Administration." Unpublished dissertation, 1951. Thomas Cooper Library, University of South Carolina, Columbia, SC.

Websites

Ancestry.com.

BattleofOlustee.org.

FindaGrave.com.

Harvard University Faculty of Arts and Sciences. "Memorial Hall/Lowell Hall Complex." www.fas.harvard.edu/~memhall/names.html.

Historical Markers of South Carolina www.scaet.org/markers.

Latitude 34 North. "Sumter County Historical Markers." http://www.lat34north.com/HistoricMarkersSC/CountyDetail.cfm?CountyNameKey=Sumter.

National Park Service. "Civil War Soldiers and Sailors Database." http://www.nps.gov/civilwar/soldiers-and-sailors-database.htm.

———. "'Comfortable Camps?': Archeology of the Confederate Guard Camp at the Florence Stockade." http://www.nps.gov/Nr/twhp/wwwlps/lessons/142Florence/142FlorenceStockade.htm.

South Carolina Division, Sons of Confederate Veterans. "Confederate Medal of Honor Recipients." http://scscv.com/confederate-past-and-present/confederate-medal-of-honor-recipients.

Terrar, Edward (Toby). "Family History Information about Charles H. Jones (1833–1891) and Elizabeth Margaret David Jones (1831–1887)." www.angelfire.com/un/joneshistory/H2-1-JON.html.

United States Army Center of Military History. "Medal of Honor Recipients—Civil War." www.history.army.mil/moh/civilwar_af.html.

University of South Carolina Society. "Experiencing History: A Visit to a Railroad 'Stonehenge.'" http://library.sc.edu/socar/uscs/newslt97/safari.html.

Index

About the Author

Historian Tom Elmore holds a BA in history and political science from the University of South Carolina. He is the author of *Columbia Civil War Landmarks* and *The Scandalous Lives of Carolina Belles Marie Boozer and Amelia Feaster: Flirting with the Enemy*, both published by The History Press, as well as *A Carnival of Destruction: Sherman's Invasion of South Carolina* and numerous articles in regional and national publications. In addition, he has lectured all across the Mid-Atlantic States. Elmore is a book reviewer for *Blue & Gray Magazine* and writes the "Columbia Gems" local history series for *Blue Fish Magazine*. He lives in Columbia with his wife, Krys, and their two Chihuahuas, Speedy and Sassy.